Profitable
Charting
Techniques

Brian J. Millard

ISBN 1 871857 03 1

Published by:

QUDOS PUBLICATIONS
16 Queensgate
Bramhall
Cheshire
SK7 1JT

Printed by Deanprint Ltd., Stockport

Profitable
Charting
Techniques

Books by the same author

Stocks and Shares Simplified
Traded Options Simplified
Channel Analysis

Contents

Preface

My previous book 'Stocks and Shares Simplified' gave the investor some basic tools with which to reduce the risk inherent in investment in the stock market. The use of moving averages figured highly as a means of establishing the turning points in share prices.

What was not discussed in that book was the importance of an analysis of patterns in share price movement. This book fills this gap, showing how such patterns are an important guide to future price movement. The way in which such patterns are derived from combinations of the various cyclical components that make up the overall share price movement is illustrated.

The investor is encouraged not to rely solely on such patterns for investment decisions. The combination of pattern analysis and the use of a variety of indicators enables the investor to focus in on the best buying and selling times.

The use of a thoroughly disciplined approach is stressed. This enables the investor to approach the ideal situation of being able to cut losses and let the profits run.

October 1990   Brian J. Millard

                                                  Bramhall

CHAPTER 1

INTRODUCTION

The subject of technical analysis, i.e. the attempt to determine future share price movements by reference to historical data, is a vast one, covering many aspects from the plotting of charts to the calculation of extremely sophisticated indicators.

This book focuses mainly on charting techniques and the operation of a few powerful indicators. The investor applying the principles discussed here will need only the simplest of tools: a pencil, ruler, eraser, pocket calculator and of course chart paper. A flexible curve or French curve that enables the smoothest curve to be drawn to pass through important high points or low points on the chart will be a useful addition. All of these items can be obtained from a High Street stationer.

For investors who are new to the idea of stock market investment, it should be pointed out that this book does not discuss how to buy and sell shares, but does discuss methods which enable the investor to arrive at buying and selling decisions. There are a number of inexpensive books on the market which discuss how to buy and sell shares, what level of dealing costs are likely to be encountered, how dividends are paid, etc. My earlier book 'Stocks and Shares Simplified' (see Appendix) covers this ground in detail, as well as moving on to ways in which shares can be selected and moving averages can be employed to reduce the risk of entering the market at the wrong time.

Investment Philosophy

Before moving to a discussion about charting techniques, it is necessary to point out to the investor the importance of maintaining a logical investment philosophy. The most important rule of investment is to preserve capital. It therefore follows that a losing position must not be held in the hope that it will soon turn around, but must be liquidated as soon as it becomes apparent that it has turned sour. On the other hand, a winning position should be maintained for as long as it continues to gain. Many investors adopt the idea of a target level for the share price, selling once the price reaches the target. This idea of creating a target level for a share price, while useful from the point of view of crystallising one's expectation for that share at the outset, must not force the investor into a premature liquidation leaving the share price to continue upwards without him.

The reader should now begin to see that the most important plank in the investment philosophy is objectivity. The investor who moves away from a purely objective approach is the investor who will start to lose money. It is not being objective to 'jump the gun' because a particular chart formation appears to be about to start. The objective investor will always wait for confirmation, and thus avoid the many occasions when the chart formation does not proceed to fruition. Before making any investment, it is vital that the investor considers the potential for gain and the potential for loss, which are perhaps better described as the 'upside potential' and the 'downside potential'. Where these are not loaded heavily in favour of the investor, the opportunity should be left alone.

The investor should also avoid being too heavily focused on just a few shares. Such an approach will have the investor seeing chart formations and opportunities which are frequently the figment of the investor's imagination. Since there are so many thousands of shares traded on the London market, then when the investor is at all uncertain about the message that the chart is giving, the motto should always be: look elsewhere for a more clear-cut picture.

One chart which it is always essential to maintain is a chart of a broad-based market index such as the All Share Index or the FTSE100 Index. The behaviour of the market as a whole can act as a useful brake on an euphoric investor who thinks he has found Eldorado all in one share. While individual shares can and do buck the trend of the market in general, this tendency to opposite behaviour is almost always short-lived. An investor needs to be extremely cautious when the market is moving adversely, and should never be afraid to admit that he has made a mistake and cut short an investment under such circumstances.

Money Management

In line with the prime requirement to preserve hard-earned capital at all costs, it is necessary to spread the risk amongst a number of shares. The larger the number of shares, the smaller the risk, while the smaller the number of shares, the greater is the risk. With too large a number of shares, the portfolio performance will tend towards boring, since the few sparkling shares will be unable to compensate for the many dull ones. With too few shares, the performance will be sparkling if the selections have been correctly selected. On the other hand the performance will be disastrous if the selections have not been correctly selected.

Thus as in most other things in life, a compromise is necessary between risk and reward. This author is of the firm opinion that about eight shares is an ideal number in which to maintain an investment. Of course, these shares are constantly changing as the investment conditions for each share changes, although it is unlikely, except when just opening a new portfolio, that the investor will be buying or selling eight shares at any one time. What will happen usually is that one or two shares will come to fruition, and the investor will be looking for new shares with which to replace them. Occasionally conditions will be such that new shares cannot be found. In such a case the money freed by share sales should be invested in a reserve, which should be a short term high interest bearing account, until such time as new opportunities occur.

From time to time the investor will make a mistake with a selection, finding that it fails to make the anticipated advance. Naturally the only course of action is to recognise the mistake and sell the share. In a typical situation, the cost of such a mistake will be of the order of 10-12% of the purchase price of the shares. About 4.5% will be necessary to cover the dealing costs of buying and selling, and the share will probably have fallen by about 5% to 10% before the investor realises that the share is not going to recover. Since only one eight of the capital is invested in such a losing share, the loss to the portfolio is one eighth of the 10-15% lost by the individual share, i.e. less than 2%. Such a loss is relatively trivial, and will easily be made up by one good winning share.

Never be tempted to decrease the number from eight shares, and never be tempted to bias the investment heavily in favour of one particular share. The investment should be reasonably close to one eighth of the available capital in each situation. Naturally, if one share does particularly well, it could come to represent considerably more than one eight of the value of the portfolio. When moving into the next share, try to maintain an even stance, committing if necessary part of the released capital from the previous share into the interest bearing account. The position can be evened up when an underperforming share is sold which requires the capital for the next investment to be topped up in order for it to continue to represent about one eighth of the value of the portfolio.

Realistic Profit Targets

Many investors, about to enter the stock market for the first time, have unrealistic expectations for the gains which can be achieved, year upon year. In a bear market, it is extremely difficult to avoid losses, let alone make any gains. In a bull market, many shares double in value over the course of a year, so that an investor with perfect timing of the buying and selling times should see a gain of 100% provided he has selected these particular shares. Most other shares will make more modest gains, perhaps of the order of 30 to 40% over the same period.

Taking an average view therefore an overall gain of say 30% after dealing costs during a year of a bull market would appear to be a more reasonable level to expect. During a bear market the investor may well be uninvested in shares since no opportunities may present themselves. In the money market therefore a gain of 10% may be the maximum obtainable. Life being what it is, most investors would be making a few investments during such a bear market, and most investors would lose possibly 10% due to the unavoidable effect of dealing costs (say about 4 to 5% for the complete buying and selling transaction) plus a loss of another 5% before any stop-loss is triggered. Thus a more realistic view of the return during a bear market may be zero percent. Since we have said that the return during a bull market is perhaps 30 to 40%, this means that for all types of market an investor would appear to be able to look forward to gains of 15 to 20%, year on year, from investment in shares. This figure would seem to be reasonable when set against the avowed aims of many institutional fund managers, which is to match the index. The index in this case is variously the FTSE100 or the All Share Index (of 750 shares). It is easy to see how such a limited aim has arisen - it can be said that a fund manager has never lost his job because he stayed level with the market. The pressure comes when a manager fails to achieve the gains made by one of these indices. On the other hand, to be fair to fund managers, they have a great deal of money to invest, money which if applied to just a few shares would heavily distort the market. They also have to operate at as low a risk as possible. Of necessity therefore they cannot behave as the small investor would do, limiting investment to just eight shares, but have to spread their investment amongst a large number of shares. This has the unavoidable effect of depressing the gain or loss towards the market average.

We can throw more light on reasonable expectations for stock market profits by looking more closely at the behaviour of the FTSE100 Index over the last six complete

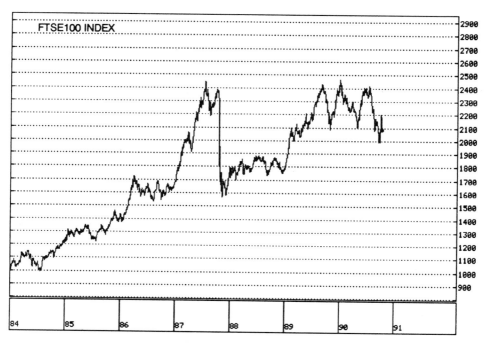

Figure 1.1. The chart of the FTSE 100 Index from the beginning of 1984.

years. Admittedly, many shares have outperformed this Index over this period of time, but equally, many shares have underperformed it. After all, the Index reflects an average view of the market, and so it is a reasonable approximation to what the average investor might have achieved. This six year chart of the FTSE100 Index is shown in Figure 1.1. The values of the Index at the beginning and end of each year, from 1984 to 1989 and the highest and lowest values reached during each year are given in Table 1.1.

These values can be used to calculate the gains made by investors who invested in a number of ways during the period. We could have an investor buying at the beginning

Table 1.1. Values of the FTSE100 Index from 1984 to 1989

Year	Start Value	End Value	Year Low	Year High
1984	997.5	1232.2	986.9	1232.2
1985	1220.0	1412.6	1206.1	1455.5
1986	1420.5	679.0	1370.1	1694.1
1987	1681.1	1712.7	1565.2	2443.4
1988	1747.5	1753.1	1694.5	1879.3
1989	1782.8	2422.7	1782.8	2423.9

Table 1.2. The Gains or Losses Made by Three Types of Buying and Selling Action During Each of the Years 1984 to 1989

Year	Buy at Beginning Sell at End	Buy at Low Sell at End	Buy at High Sell at End
1984	23.5	24.9	0
1985	15.8	17.1	-2.9
1986	18.2	22.5	-0.9
1987	1.8	9.4	-29.9
1988	2.6	5.8	-4.6
1989	35.9	35.9	-0.1
Averages	16.3	19.3	-6.4

of the year and selling at the end of that year, or we could have an investor buying at the low point for that year and selling at the end of the year, and finally we could have an unfortunate investor who bought at the high point for the year and sold at the end of the year. The gains or losses made by these actions are shown in Table 1.2.

During each of the six years the market has finished higher at the end of the year than at the beginning, with the average gain for a year being 16.3%. An investor who correctly identified the low point for the year would have seen an average increase of 19.3%, while an investor who incorrectly bought at the high point for the year and sold at the end of the year would have made an average loss of 6.4%.

This helps to put the stock market into perspective, and shows that gains of about 20% year on year are realistic for an investor who is able to achieve fairly good timing of the buying and selling points for his shares. An above average investor who is able to pick consistently the shares which outperform the market may make gains of up to 30% year on year, but such investors are scarce.

The impact of dealing costs on stock market gains should not be ignored. In very round figures, for a deal of say £1000, an investor can expect buying costs of about £25 and selling costs of about £20. This is equivalent to a total of 4.5%. For an investor who remains invested for long periods of time, more than one year, in a particular share, these dealing costs will be offset for the most part by the dividends which are received. It is the short term investor, who stays with a share for just a few weeks or months, who suffers most from dealing costs, since he is probably not invested in the share at the time when a dividend is due.

On the other hand, the short term investor gains markedly from the compounding effect of being able to re-invest the proceeds of one transaction immediately into the next. Even quite small average gains per transaction grow quite rapidly into large annual gains. This is shown quite clearly in Table 1.3, where the typical gain, after dealing costs

Table 1.3. Cumulative gains for increasing numbers of trades per year.

No. of trades per annum	% Gain per trade assuming 100% rise over year	% Gain per trade adjusted for dealing costs	Cumulative gain per annum if reinvested
1	100	95.5	95.5
2	50	45.5	111.7
4	25	20.5	110.6
6	16.6	12.1	98.4
12	8.3	3.8	56.4

for transactions of increasingly shorter time is listed, along with the equivalent annual gain for re-investment of the proceeds of each transaction in the next one. It can be seen that gains after dealing costs of 3.8% for transactions lasting just a month still accumulate into 56% for the year. The Table also shows that there is no substantial difference between an investor who buys and holds for a year before selling and the investors who hold for six months, three months or two months, since they all appear to achieve gains of between 90% and 111%. However, as presented here for simplicity in using round percentage gains, the Table is biased in favour of the long term investor, who has been given a nominal gain of 100%, with the other gains being adjusted on a pro-rata basis of half of this over six months, a quarter over three months, etc.

In practice, a gain of 100% over one transaction lasting one year will be difficult to obtain, whereas a gain of say 30% over three months will be much easier. This is because of the way in which shares move; they tend to put on their gains over a short period of time. Shares go through periods where their rate of gain is quite high, periods where they remain more or less static, and periods where their rate of loss is quite high. This will become more apparent when we look at charts later. The effect of this behaviour is that the high rate of gain is usually compressed into about a three month period. This is a good average length of time for which an investor should remain invested in any particular share, and with good timing and good share selection, it should be possible to frequently capture gains of up to 30% in such a period. Allowing for the number of occasions when the timing is not good, an investor who has become an expert at charting techniques should be able to make a gain of about 15% over each three month period during good market conditions. When compounded into the next transaction, gains of 15% each three months become 74% over the year.

As stated previously, during bad market conditions the investor will be unable to do much better than the interest which can be made by putting his capital into the money market. Looked at in this way, the good gains which can be made during good markets have to compensate for the standstill position during bad markets.

The Use of a Stop Loss

It might seem to be a rather negative approach to bring in a discussion of methods of avoiding losses at this stage of the book. After all, investment books should have as their objective the making of money through correct investment technique. This is of course the aim of this book, but it is an indisputable fact that more money is lost by investors who fail to sell at the correct time than is lost by investors who buy at the wrong time. All of the gains made by the correct application of the chartist techniques discussed in this book can be lost if the investor fails to act when the trend turns against him. It is therefore essential that the investor operates a stop loss system, and it is discussed this early in the book in order to bring home the overriding importance of this.

A stop loss is a price level below the current share price which the investor sets as the lowest point to which he is prepared to see the share price fall. A fall of the price below this stop loss must immediately trigger the investor to sell, with no ifs and buts. The stop loss method is therefore an automatic one, and the investor must not negate its use by sometimes failing to act on it because of a gut feeling that the share price will recover. All such gut feelings should have been taken into account when the stop loss level is originally set. The term 'stop loss' should more properly be called 'rising stop loss' since as the share price rises, the stop loss level is also raised, so that the price gain becomes built into the stop loss system. The stop loss should never be lowered.

The setting of a stop loss level is a balancing act between two basic requirements. Firstly there is the need to maximise the profit already built into the share price by virtue of a rise since the share was bought, which means of course that the effect of a fall has to be minimised. Secondly there is the need to avoid premature exit from the share which then may continue upwards without the investor. If share prices just went up in a straight line and then turned around and fell in an equally straight line, then the operation of a stop loss would be simplicity itself: the level would be set at a point fractionally below the current share price. Unfortunately, prices do not behave like that. Because of the existence of short term, medium term and long term trends, plus a degree of random movement, prices move up and down in zig-zags. If zigs are taken to be larger moves than zags, then the stop loss is intended to allow upward zigs to run their course, accommodate the downward zags, but protect against downward zags that turn into downward zigs. This is illustrated in Figure 1.2.

The crucial decision about a stop loss is the distance below the current share price at which to set it. If the level is set too close to the current share price, then the stop loss is triggered by a small zag in the price, so that the investor has then lost out on the succeeding rise (Figure 1.2 upper). If the level is set too far below the current share price, then the stop loss fails to be triggered until the zag has become an extensive downward zig, so causing the investor a loss that is much bigger than is acceptable (Figure 1.2 lower). The correct setting of the stop loss allows the investor to take in his stride the inevitable small downward zags in the share price, leaves him invested for the larger upward moves and makes sure that he is protected against a fall that is more than just a small downward zag.

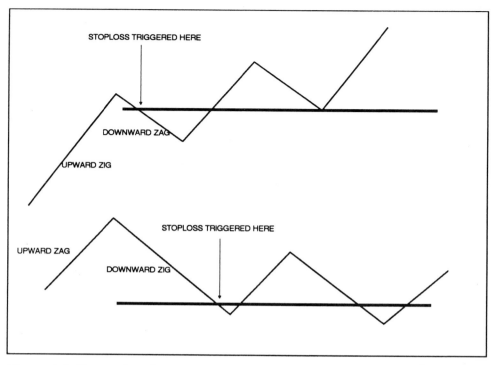

Figure 1.2. Upper: Stop loss set too close to the rising price gives a premature sell signal on a small downward correction. **Lower:** Stop loss set too far below rising price allows an appreciable loss to occur before giving sell signal. Note: zigs are small price changes while zags are larger price changes in either direction.

There are two basic systems of stop loss which can be used, one which is based on a floor which is a constant amount, e.g. 10 pence below the rising price. The other one is based on a floor which is a constant percentage below the rising price.

Constant amount stop loss

The major advantage of a constant amount stop loss is that only the simplest of calculation is required - subtraction. As the price rises, the constant amount is subtracted from the share price. Thus for a 10p stop loss, if the share price is at 340p, then the stop loss is at 330p. If the share price rises the following day to 345p, then the stop loss is raised to 335p. On the other hand if the price falls, for example to 331p, then the stop loss stays where it is at 330p. If the price then falls to 329p the time has come to sell.

Thus the operation of the constant amount stop loss is simplicity itself. The real work comes in deciding whether the constant amount should be 10p, 12p, 20p or some other value. There is no requirement that the constant amount should be a nice round number such as 10p or 15p, and there is no relationship between the constant amount which is optimum for one share and that which may be the best for another share. A value such as 16.5p may turn out to be the best value for a particular set of circumstances.

The constant amount can only be determined by study of the past behaviour of the share price itself. The best way is to look at the chart of the share price and look at an upwards trend which is reasonably comparable with the expectations you have for the current uptrend. Then make a note of the extent of each of the minor falls during the course of the extended rise. If the values lie close together, so much the better, since the constant stop loss may be acceptable if it is set at a value only slightly greater than the largest of these falls. There is more difficulty if the falls cover quite a range of values, since the larger of these may represent a fall which is quite unacceptable if the share price does not recover. Thus a compromise is often inevitable between the historical minor corrections in the share price and the amount of loss which the investor feels he can tolerate.

Having decided on a value for the constant amount, the investor should try this value on various parts of the share price history to see if the results obtained are satisfactory. If they are not, adjust the level slightly and try again.

Once the investor has carried out this process on a few shares, the experience obtained will make it much easier to decide on good values for other shares.

Constant percentage stop loss

The world of investment is a world of percentages, so it is not surprising that many investors favour a stop loss system which is based on a floor a fixed percentage down from the rising price. I do not favour this method for two reasons. Firstly the calculation is slightly more awkward than for the constant amount stop loss, especially as the floor level calculated will still have to be rounded off to the nearest whole or perhaps half a pence. Secondly a study of a large number of share price movements will show that the minor falls during the lifetime of a longer term uptrend tend not to increase in their value in pence as the share price rises, i.e. the falls are based on an absolute amount rather than a percentage amount. Thus it seems conceptually incorrect to use a percentage method for a share price movement situation which is not based on percentages.

As was discussed for the constant amount stop loss, the percentage value to be used can only be discovered by trial and error on the past history of the share price. For most shares, a value of around 3% to 4% will be found to give acceptable results, in the sense that the investor would not be shaken out of the share too frequently. Most investors would also be pleased to get out of a falling price only 3 or 4% down from the peak.

CHAPTER 2

Charts and Indicators

In this chapter we will discuss the various types of charts which can be constructed and the simple indicators which can be calculated readily with the minimum of effort by the investor. The large number of more complex indicators, many of which require computer calculations, are more properly the subject of a wider ranging book on technical analysis. The chart types which will be considered are linear, semilogarithmic, Point and Figure and Rise-fall. The indicators which will be discussed are moving averages, the Relative Strength Indicator and the Welles Wilder Relative Strength Indicator. Each of these indicators fall into the category of calculated indicators, i.e. it is necessary to use the exact numerical values of the share price data at intervals such as daily or weekly to compute a numerical value for the indicator. The rise-fall indicator is a special case, since it is based on a trendline superimposed on the rise-fall chart, and thus needs no numerical computation.

Linear Charts

These are the simplest to understand and the easiest to plot. A linear chart has scales which are equally divided, so that a fixed distance along either the vertical price scale or the horizontal time scale is always equivalent to the same change in price or the same number of days or weeks of elapsed time. Before setting out to construct such a linear chart, the investor has to make two decisions. Firstly for how long is the chart going to be maintained, and secondly over what price range is the share price expected to move during the period for which the chart is going to be kept?

Linear chartpaper as bought either loosely or in pads at a stationers will have two sets of graduations. The larger scale ones are heavy lines, and between these are fainter lines which represent divisions of tenths of the distance between successive pairs of heavy lines. The charts can be metric or imperial. In the first case the distance between heavy lines is one centimetre and between faint lines is therefore one millimetre, while for the imperial the distance between heavy lines is one inch and between faint lines one tenth of an inch. Since an inch is approximately 2.5 cms, there are two and a half times as many lines in each direction on an A4 sheet of metric graph paper compared with an A4 sheet of imperial graph paper. A metric sheet is usually ruled into a grid of 18 cms by 26 cms, giving 180 divisions by 260 divisions. An imperial sheet is usually ruled into a grid of 7.5 inches by 11 inches, giving 75 divisions by 110 divisions.

Which of these two types of graph paper is appropriate depends upon what the investor is trying to determine from the charts. For short term movements the metric chart will cover 110 days or weeks if the longer axis is used for the time. The larger separation of the graduations will make this type of chart easier to read, and for short term periods will possibly be the better of the two. The metric chart will keep the investor going for 260 days, i.e. one year if used for daily data, or five years of weekly data, and therefore is more appropriate for viewing the bigger picture of share price movement.

Where the investor requires more thought is in the way in which the vertical price axis is to be labelled. The range should take into account reasonable expectation for the range over which the share price will move over the ensuing time period, and should include plenty of room for a fall from the starting point as well as enough room for a projected rise.

From the typical metric graph paper we have one hundred and eighty vertical divisions, while for imperial paper there will be usually seventy five. The distance between heavy horizontal lines should be taken as a number which is readily divisible by ten, and not some awkward value which will make it less easy to plot intermediate values.

The major advantage of linear charts is their simplicity, since the same distance on the chart paper always represents the same difference in price or time. However, they do suffer from some disadvantages. Thus they do not allow the investor to compare percentage changes as easily as the semilogarithmic variety. They also do not accommodate unexpected surges or falls in the share price, which will then run off the top or bottom of the chart, necessitating the complete redrawing to a different scale. On the other hand, as will be seen from the chapter on Channel Analysis, cyclical features in share price movement tend to be based on a constant amplitude, so that it is easy to draw channels of constant depth on linear paper. This becomes almost impossible on semilog charts.

Semilogarithmic Charts

Semilogarithmic charts have the same linear scale in one direction as linear charts, and since time is a linear function, then obviously the linear axis will be used as the time axis. It is in the vertical price direction that the two types of chart differ. The logarithmic scale has the property that a certain distance on the chart represents a constant ratio. Thus the distance apart of the points for say 100p and 200p on the price axis is the same distance as that between the points for 200p and 400p. Because of this, semilog charts have the useful feature that percentage change on them remains constant up the vertical scale. Thus if the underlying semilog grid is the same for the charts of two different shares even though the price marks on the grids may be different, then they can be directly compared from the point of view of percentage change at any moment in time. This is very useful where it is necessary to compare two investments.

One difficulty with logarithmic charts which limits their use with certain indicators is that zero and negative values have no meaning. They cannot be expressed on a logarithmic scale. For straightforward share charts this of course is not a problem.

Semilogarithmic chart paper has one further specification - the number of cycles on the logarithmic scale. This simply means how many times the scale runs from 1 to 10. A single cycle would have ten heavy lines, getting closer together as they run up to the top of the paper. A two cycle log paper would have the first cycle running from lines 1 to 10, the tenth being halfway up the paper, while the next cycle would start from line ten and run up to another tenth line.

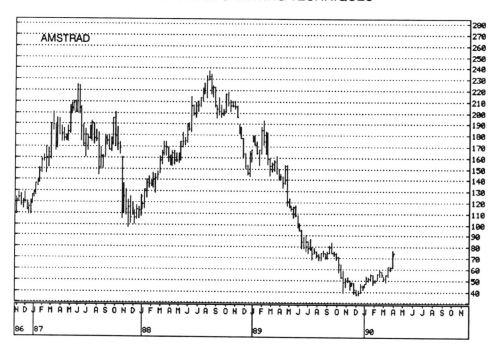

Figure 2.1. A weekly bar chart of the Amstrad share price on a linear scale.

If the heavy lines are labelled with prices, then single cycle paper would take the price up to a factor of ten times the price marked at the first graduation, while two cycle paper would take it up to a hundred times. Naturally for share price movement, even a factor of ten is usually excessive, so that single cycle semilogarithmic paper will be perfectly adequate for share price charting.

As with linear scales, the investor will have to think carefully about the range to be used for the price scale. As stated above, it will cover a factor of ten between the first and last values. The scale should start at a point comfortably below the current starting price in order to accommodate a fall in price without the necessity of redrawing the chart. If the current price is in the low 200p level, then 100p to 1000p would be sensible markings for the price scale. If the price is 500p, then 200p to 2000p would be obvious graduations to use. Note that the scale markings are multiples of the price at the first scale mark. Thus if this is 200, the next mark is 400, the next 600 and so on up to 2000. It is important to avoid numbers that cannot easily be divided by 10, since it will then be difficult to interpolate intermediate points on the fine grid lines. Thus 6, 8, 16 are not good values, while 5 and 25, while not multiples of 10, are easily subdivided into 0.5 and 0.25.

Many commercial charts, on close examination, consist of small vertical bars. This is particularly true of American charts. Often there is a small cross line horizontally through the vertical bar. These vertical bars are simply the range over which the share has traded during the day (or week for weekly charts). The lowest part of the bar is at a

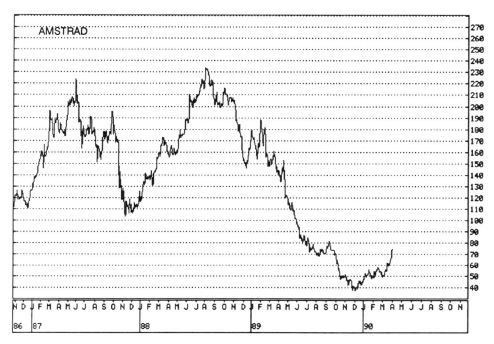

Figure 2.2. A line chart of the Amstrad daily share price on a linear scale.

point corresponding to the lowest point, and the top of the bar of course is at the highest point. The cross line indicates the level at which the share price closed. Occasionally this might also be the highest price or lowest for the day.

For the amateur chartist, it is difficult to get at the daily range values without subscribing to an electronic feed of data to a personal computer or to the Stock Exchange Daily Official List. For this reason almost all amateurs plot just the closing price, or the closing price as it appears in the next day's newspaper. The point is plotted by drawing a line from the last plotted point to the current one. Such a chart is called a line plot, as opposed to the bar chart described above for daily ranges.

Examples of bar and line charts in both linear and semilogarithmic form are shown in Figure 2.1 to 2.4. Note that movement is much less obvious in the semilogarithmic charts than the linear charts because of the dampening effect of showing price changes as ratio changes as opposed to differences.

The chartist has the option of plotting daily or weekly values. Quite obviously there is five times as much work involved in daily plotting as opposed to weekly plotting. The best procedure is to carry weekly plots of the pool of shares which you are monitoring as the source of future investment opportunities. As a share approaches a point at which an investment opportunity seems imminent, then switch to maintaining a daily chart in addition to the weekly chart. In this way the amount of work is kept to a minimum. Note

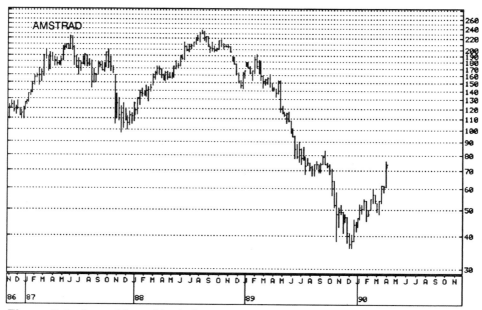

Figure 2.3. A semi-logarithmic bar chart of the Amstrad share price.

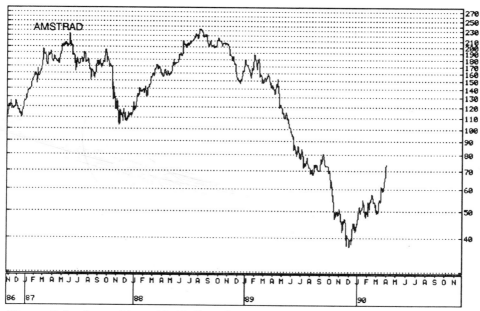

Figure 2.4. A semi-logarithmic line chart of the Amstrad share price.

that daily charts should be kept for all shares in which you are currently invested, as well as those for shares in which you hope to invest shortly.

Point and Figure Charts

These are not as popular in the United Kingdom as they are in the United States. It is important that investors at least get a feel for what they mean, so they are described here so that investors will be able to construct their own if they wish.

The horizontal axis on normal charts is the time axis, and as such is equally divided into daily or weekly time intervals. Even if the share price remains fixed at a constant value for days or weeks on end, a point will still be plotted at the corresponding point in time. Point and figure (P&F) charts are quite different, since the horizontal axis is not a time axis. If the price does not change, no point is plotted on the chart. Because points are only plotted if there is price movement, P&F charts are a measure of the activity in the share in question.

Point and figure charts have a linear vertical scale, but unlike normal charts where a horizontal line corresponds to a price, it is the gap between the lines that corresponds to a price value in P&F charts. P&F charts are characterised by one further quantity - the box reversal. The most usual value is a three-box reversal, but the value can be anything from one box upwards. The higher the number of boxes the less sensitive is the chart to price movement. Hence the one-box reversal type is the most sensitive.

It is conventional, though not strictly necessary, to use X's for a rising price and O's for a falling price. This makes it rather easier to read the charts. As an example, the way of plotting a one-box reversal P&F chart is now described.

The first thing to decide is the value of a box. This will depend upon the level of the share price. If the price is in the range of say 100 to 200p then a box could have a value of 5p. At the starting point in time, nothing will be put on the chart until the price has moved either up or down from that value. Supposing the starting point is 150p. Since the value of a box is 5p, the price has to move by that amount before any mark can be put on the chart. A movement of 4p up or down will not be plotted. If the price rises to 155p, or indeed any value between 155 and 159p then an X is put opposite the 155p level. If the price falls by this amount, an O is put instead, but this time of course opposite the 145p level. Because the value of a box is 5p, the actual price movement is rounded to the nearest multiple of 5p downward for a rise and upward for a fall. For a rising price, X's are put in all of the boxes up to that rounded value, and for a falling price O's are put in all of the boxes down to the rounded level.

Now we do not keep putting X's and O's in the same column, since this would give little information about the share price movement. Since the type of chart being plotted is called a one-box reversal, we move to the next column to the right when the price movement changes direction. We put our X or O one box up or one box down from the previous last entry in the previous column. We still have to fill in boxes with either X's or O's as appropriate up to or down to the new price level which is reached. For example, supposing the price has been falling so that the current column has a number of O's in it down to the box corresponding to 120p. If the price then moves up to 136p, we move one column to the right, put an X in the box corresponding to 125p (but not in the one corresponding to 120p) and then further X's in the boxes for 130p and 135p. If the price

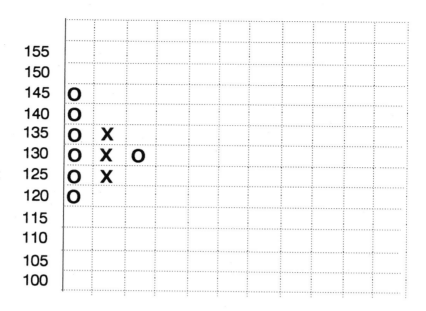

Figure 2.5. How a Point and Figure chart is constructed. The box and reversal size is 5p. Only movements of 5p or greater will be plotted. Price falls are represented by O's and price rises by X's. Following a fall to 120p in the first column, a subsequent rise to 136p results in X's being placed as shown. Finally a fall to 129p results in an O being placed in the 130p box.

then moves down to 129p, we move one column again to the right and put an O in the box corresponding to 130p. The result of these few moves in the price is shown in Figure 2.5.

When the price direction changes again we move again to the next column. We can now see that the greater the number of changes in the direction of the share price, the faster does the chart creep across the chart paper.

The one-box reversal P&F charts are too responsive to price changes to be of any great use in share price analysis. Because of this a three-box reversal is much more common. The principle is exactly the same as for a one-box reversal. You move to the next column when the price changes direction and by an amount greater than the value of three boxes. However, while the price is continuing in the same direction you continue to plot movements corresponding to one box. It is the reversal that has to be three boxes, while the continuation in the same direction stays at one box.

Reading Point and Figure Charts

In Figure 2.6 is shown the three-box reversal chart of P&O. The letters and numbers at the ends of each column give the month and the last digit of the year when the price

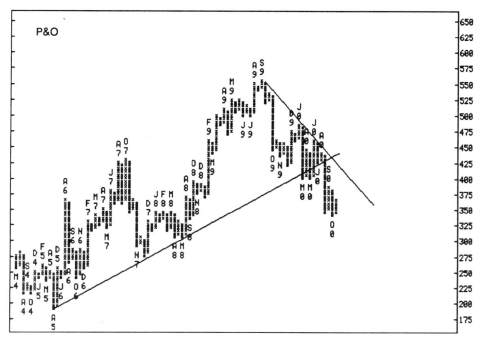

Figure 2.6. A Point and Figure chart of P&O. A 3 box reversal has been used. The time of occurrence of reversals is indicated by the month letter and last digit of the year. Thus the latest reversal (into a rising trend) is in October 1990. As with normal charts, trendlines can be drawn as shown in this example.

reversal occurred. Thus A0 is August 1990. Trendlines can be drawn on P&F charts just as on normal charts, and two such lines are shown in Figure 2.6. The uptrend was broken by the long fall which occurred in August 1990. The downtrend line has yet to be penetrated on the upside, and so it appears that at the time of writing P&O shares are not yet ready for a rise.

Rise-Fall Charts

These are a third way of presenting share price data which is extremely valuable for determining changes in the direction of the share price which are signalled by penetration of trend lines.

Normal charts have a price axis and a time axis, Point and Figure charts have a price axis but no time axis, while rise-fall charts have a time axis but no price axis. The vertical axis is a direction indicator, and its graduations are a measure of the length of time that a share price direction has continued.

It is the simplest possible chart to construct, and requires a linear chart paper. This is a case where the millimetric divisions on metric chart paper are probably too closely spaced, so that imperial paper graduated in tenths of an inch is much more appropriate. If metric chart paper is used, movement will be much easier to study if two millimetre graduations are used to represent one movement.

Figure 2.7. The Rise-fall chart of BICC from late 1989. The chart is constructed by taking an arbitrary starting number such as 100 and increasing it by 1 unit if the price has risen from the previous day, decreasing it by 1 if the price has fallen, and leaving it unchanged if the price is unchanged. Buying and selling points are determined by the breaking of trend lines.

The horizontal axis should be marked as the time scale, either daily or weekly depending upon the lengths of trends which are being studied. Put the first point halfway up the vertical axis exactly on a horizontal line. For the next data point, if the price moves upwards, draw a line from the previous point up one graduation and across one graduation to the current date. If the price falls, draw a line from the previous point down one graduation and across to the current date. If the price is unchanged, draw a horizontal line from the previous point to the current date.

Thus the rise-fall chart takes no notice of the size of a rise or fall, but only that a rise or fall has occurred. An immediate picture is given of the length of time for which upward, downward or sideways trends persist. As will be seen later, the breaking of trend lines gives a very powerful method of early detection of the end of an uptrend or a downtrend. An example of a rise fall chart is shown in Figure 2.7 for BICC.

Numerical Indicators

Indicators are primarily used as an aid to the identification of the beginning of a new directional trend. Most indicators are numerical quantities that can be calculated from the share price data, others require some other source of data, such as the number of shares which rise or fall each day or week, and some, such as the rise-fall indicator require no calculation. The indicators discussed in this section are of the type which are easily calculated from the share price itself. They are very widely used, indeed in the case of moving averages universally used, and have stood the test of time.

Moving Averages

The vast majority of amateur chartists, and indeed many professionals, use moving averages without having the least idea of their mathematical properties. These mathematical properties are indeed very simple, but understanding them will bring a more objective approach to the use of moving averages in chart analysis.

Moving averages are 'better' representations of the share price itself. They remove what might be called 'noise' from the share price movement. The type of noise which is removed depends upon which span is used to calculate the average. The span is simply the number of points which are averaged. Thus a 9-day moving average is obtained by adding the prices for 9 successive days and dividing by 9. The span of this average is 9. The term 'moving' is used because the investor moves through the available price data continually adding up the last 9 prices and dividing by 9. Thus with say eleven daily prices available, a 9-day moving average would have three values. The first nine prices when averaged give the first of these averaged points, the nine values starting with the second price and ending with the last price but one will give the second average point, and finally starting with the third price and ending with the last price gives the final, third value of the moving average.

The above method of calculating an average is long-winded, and one can imagine the amount of effort required in calculating a 200-day moving average for say five years of daily data. The process can be greatly simplified by keeping a running total. How this is done for the BICC share price between 1st June 1990 and 21st June 1990 is shown in Table 2.1 for a 9-day average. Five columns are required to carry out the calculation. The first column contains the date, the second the daily or weekly prices, the next column is a reminder of which values to add to and subtract from the running total, the next column is the running total and the final column is the average, obtained by dividing the value in the running total column by the span of the average, in this case nine.

Adding up the first nine values gives a total of 4079. This is put in the fourth column on the ninth line down, i.e. in this case opposite the 13th June. Dividing this by nine gives the value of the average, 453.22 which is put alongside the total in the final column. Now to calculate the next value of the average, it is not necessary to add up a further nine values starting from the price on the 4th June. Instead we add in the next price in the list, i.e. the tenth value on the 14th June (458), and subtract the tenth price back from this point, i.e. the first value we used on the 1st June (443). This gives us a new total of 4094, which is put below the previous one. Dividing by nine gives the corresponding average, 454.88 which is put in the last column. The use of the third column now become apparent. It is to enable you to remember which value has has been dropped. Since the first value has been dropped, we put a cross in the first line in this column. The next time we do the calculation we will see that it is the second value which has to be dropped from the running total. Thus to the new total of 4094 we add in the next price of 453 and drop the price on the next line after the cross, i.e. 449 to give a new total of 4098 and a new average of 455.33. We then put our cross below the previous one.

Table 2.1. Calculation of a 9-day moving average.

Date	Price	Subtract	Total	Average
01/06/90	443	X		
04/06/90	449	X		
05/06/90	451	X		
06/06/90	451	X		
07/06/90	462	X		
08/06/90	455	X		
11/06/90	450			
12/06/90	458			
13/06/90	460		4079	453.22
14/06/90	458		4094	454.88
15/06/90	453		4098	455.33
18/06/90	450		4097	455.22
19/06/90	449		4095	455
20/06/90	452		4085	453.88
21/06/90	455		4085	453.88

We proceed in this manner until all the prices have been used up, so that we will have a running total and an average value alongside the last price in the list.

Obviously for averages with longer spans, such as 200 day, we will have much more work in calculating the first average value, but after that, we simply have one addition, one subtraction and one division to provide us with subsequent values of the average.

Note that Saturday and Sunday dates are omitted. Only business days, when the Stock Exchange carried out business, are used for the moving average calculations. There are differences of opinion on how Bank Holidays should be treated. It is best to put down the same value as on the previous working day, on the basis that a price stays the same until changed by the market.

We mentioned that moving averages remove noise from the original data, and that the type of noise removed depends upon the span of the average. A moving average will remove all fluctuations in the data with a frequency equal to or less than the span of the average, and allow through fluctuations greater than the span of the average. Thus a nine day average would remove the random day-to-day variations in the share price and any fluctuations which are based on underlying cycles of movement which repeat themselves every nine days or less. Since variations of ten days or upwards would still come through, a nine day average is only moderately smooth, still showing the presence of short term, medium term and long term variations. In this context short term would apply to variations with a cyclicality of between about ten days and thirty days, medium term would apply to variations of between thirty one days and two hundred days, and any variations over 200 days would be considered to be long term.

The values for spans which are used by various chartists can now be put into perspective. A 200-day moving average is common, and from the above comments we can see that its value is in removing short and medium term fluctuations, leaving the underlying long term trend visible. Thus it is sensible to avoid investment in a share when the 200-day average, and hence the long term trend, is falling. Also common are ten-day and twenty-day averages, often used together, and here it is the short term and medium term trends that are being highlighted. These are appropriate to those investors who wish to take advantage of short term trends and who recognise the higher risk involved.

It is useful to keep two averages at the same time. In this case three other columns should be added to the table for each additional average: one for the subtract column, one for the running total for that average, and one for the average itself. Although as mentioned above, 10-day and 20-day averages are frequently used together, two averages are of much more value if they are much wider apart. Thus a 10-day average and a 200-day average can serve to throw light on both short term and long term underlying trends.

Plotting Averages on Charts

In Chapter 10, where moving averages are discussed, we shall see that averages are viewed as 'better' or smoother versions of the share price data itself. As such, they have to be plotted half a span back in time, which is the correct mathematical method of using them. However, the earliest chartists, who were in no way mathematicians, started plotting them incorrectly, and the practice has persisted so long that it is now not possible to eradicate it. The chartist way of plotting averages is with no lag, i.e. they are plotted exactly as they fall in a calculation such as that shown in Table 2.1. The value for an average is plotted at the same point in time as the last data point used for the calculation. Referring again to Table 2.1, this means that the average value of 453.22 would be plotted at the time corresponding to the 13th June 1990. When plotted this way, movement of the average will lag behind movement in the share price, i.e. if the share price turns up from a falling mode, the average will take some time to respond and itself turn up from a falling mode. The larger the span of the average, the longer is this gap between the two events.

There are two basic ways in which averages are used in normal charting techniques. One method is to wait until the price moves above the average before buying and conversely wait until the price fall below the average before selling. The other way is to wait until the average itself changes direction. A reversal to a rising trend is a signal to buy, while a change to a downward trend is a signal to sell. The correctness of either method as a generator of buying or selling signals is extremely sensitive to the span of the average being used. Actual examples of the use of moving averages are given in Chapter 10.

Relative Strength Index (RSI)

This is also a widely used index, and in the UK is taken to mean the ratio of a share price to a broadly based market index such as the FT All Share Index. It should not be

Table 2.2. The Relative Strength Index for BICC versus the FTSE100 Index.

Date	Price	FTSE100	Ratio:Price/FTSE100
01/06/90	443	2371.4	0.1868
04/06/90	449	2379.0	0.1887
05/06/90	451	2380.1	0.1895
06/06/90	451	2358.5	0.1912
07/06/90	462	2378.4	0.1942
08/06/90	455	2366.6	0.1923
11/06/90	450	2348.8	0.1916
12/06/90	458	2370.7	0.1932
13/06/90	460	2405.4	0.1912
14/06/90	458	2403.0	0.1906
15/06/90	453	2392.3	0.1894
18/06/90	450	2392.3	0.1881
19/06/90	449	2370.5	0.1894
20/06/90	452	2371.2	0.1906
21/06/90	455	2370.3	0.1920

confused with the Welles Wilder Relative Strength Index, which in this book we have simply called the Welles Wilder Index. In commercial charts, the RSI is superimposed on the lower third of the share price chart, or sometimes in its own box below the main chart.

Because this indicator is a ratio, it will increase as a share moves higher relative to the market, and decrease as a share moves lower relative to the market. As can be seen from examples, its main use for investors is to enable them to focus on shares which are outperforming the market in general, and to avoid those shares which are underperforming the market.

The RSI is easily calculated each day or week by dividing the share price by the index, which is can be the All share Index, or the FTSE100 Index. This is shown in Table 2.2 for BICC between the dates 1st June 1990 and 21st June 1990 using the FTSE100 Index as the divisor.

With the All Share Index around the 1100 mark at the time of writing, and the FTSE100 around 2300, values can run from say 0.005 for penny shares up to about 1 for shares which are trading at around the 10. Obviously these cannot be plotted directly on a chart which may have scales running from 10 to 1000. Either the values have to be adjusted by some constant factor, or more easily, a different scale can used on the existing chart. Investors are mostly interested in whether the RSI is rising or falling, so actual values of the RSI are of secondary importance to direction as seen on a chart. The scale for the RSI should be such as to restrict the plot of this indicator to the bottom of the chart, but should be wide enough that the movements are not crowded into a very small area. A crowded RSI makes it difficult to absorb the message from it.

The Welles Wilder Index

This indicator is among the group called momentum indicators. These indicators are looking at the rate at which a share price is changing; the higher the rate of change the greater the momentum. From this the deduction is that the greater the momentum of the share price, the less likely is it to change direction. The best analogy is with a vehicle moving forward which has to stop before moving in reverse. Initially it has a large momentum which decreases as the brakes are applied. Before moving backwards in reverse it will have a zero momentum, even if this condition holds for a fraction of a second. As it accelerates away in reverse, the momentum will increase again in the opposite direction. Thus a fall in momentum to zero or almost zero is the signal that the direction is about to change.

The indicator developed by J. Welles Wilder groups prices into rising prices and falling prices. Just as in the case of the span required for a moving average calculation, a period is chosen over which to calculate the indicator. This is usually 14 days, although other periods may be useful in certain circumstances. All the price rises during the first

Table 2.3. Calculation of the Welles Wilder Index.

Date	Price	Rise	Fall	Total Rises in 14 days	Total Falls in 14 days	UP/DOWN	WW
01/06/90	443						
04/06/90	449	6					
05/06/90	451	2					
06/06/90	451	0					
07/06/90	462	9					
08/06/90	455		7				
11/06/90	450		5				
12/06/90	458	8					
13/06/90	460	2					
14/06/90	458		2				
15/06/90	453		5				
18/06/90	450		3				
19/06/90	449		1				
20/06/90	452	3					
21/06/90	455	3		30	23	1.30	56.59

fourteen day period are added together to give a quantity which we can call UP. All the price falls during the same period are added to give a quantity which we can call DOWN.

The Welles Wilder Indicator is then 100-(100/(1 + (UP/DOWN)))

As an example, the indicator is calculated for the BICC share price over the same period of time as was used for the moving average calculation. This is shown in Table 2.3. The first entry for the 1st June 1990 is required only to establish the rise for the next day. The 14 day period then runs from the 4th June to the 21st June. Each day the price change from the previous day is noted as a rise or a fall. The total of the rises during the 14 day period is then 30p, and the total of the falls is then 23p. The quantity UP/DOWN is 30/23 = 1.304. Thus the WW value is:

$$100 - (100/(1 + 1.304)) = 100 \text{-} (100/2.304) = 56.6$$

The way in which the indicator is calculated means that its value always lies between 0 and 100. This makes it easy to scale onto a share price chart. Another useful aspect of this indicator is that the UP and DOWN parts of the computation have been averaged, and therefore this makes the indicator less liable to react to very short term fluctuations.

The indicator is used by drawing horizontal lines on the chart at the levels corresponding to 70 and 30 (some chartists use 75 and 25). When the indicator moves above 70 it is considered to be overbought, while a fall below 30 means it is considered to be oversold. Although some investors sell as soon as the indicator moves above the 70 mark, and sell as soon as it moves below 30, most chartists wait until the indicator has peaked if it rises above 70, or troughed if it falls below 30. A few chartists adopt the approach of carrying out the appropriate action once the indicator has been above 70 or below 30 for a particular number of days.

Usually the Welles Wilder indicator is a leading indicator, i.e. it gives its signal before the share price changes direction, whereas the moving average gives its signal after the price changes direction. Moving averages can therefore be considered to be lagging averages, which act in the confirmatory sense that the change in direction has occurred.

As well as using the indicator in the sense discussed above, where it signals overbought and oversold levels, it also generates chart patterns of the same type as normal price charts, and therefore the same chartist techniques can be applied to the plots of the indicator.

The use of the indicator will be covered in Chapter 11.

CHAPTER 3

Trends Within Trends

Share price movement is a complex mixture of trends – very short term, short term, medium term, long term and very long term. In this context a trend is simply a direction of movement. Thus there are uptrends and downtrends and occasionally sideways trends. As a starting point for consideration of the nature of trends, a chart of the BICC share price over about one month is shown in Figure 3.1, a chart of one year of the price movement is shown in Figure 3.2, while in Figure 3.3 is shown seven years of the price movement.

Taking Figure 3.1 first of all, it can be seen quite clearly that the share price is moving up and down almost on a daily basis. Underneath this day to day variation, it can be seen that after a few days the price has begun a movement which takes it up to its highest point for the month at about the middle of the chart. Thus it can be said that this first half of one month's price history shows the existence of an uptrend, which has taken the price from 258p to 290p over the course of ten trading days. This uptrend co-exists with the day to day up and down movements, which in themselves, if they last for more than one day, can be considered to be mini-uptrends and downtrends. From that halfway point, the price declines again, ending the period at 261p. Thus there is now in existence a downtrend. Both the uptrend and the downtrend appear to have been completed within the time range covered by the chart.

Thus this first chart has shown us the existence of uptrends and downtrends of such a short duration, just a few days, that they are useless from the point of view of investment. It has also shown us the existence of an uptrends which lasts for about ten days plus a downtrend of similar duration.

This view of just one month's price history gives us no idea of where the price may be headed over the following year. This is because the slice of history is much too short to identify the longer term trends which will take the price onwards for such a length of time. This is put right by the longer, one year piece of history shown in Figure 3.2. The peak price of 290p attained in Figure 3.1 can now be seen at the right hand side of the chart for the month of November 1986. Now we can see the existence of more of the short term trends such as those discussed for Figure 3.1, and in addition medium term trends are clearly visible. One such medium term trend is already in being at the point where the chart commences in December 1985, and this trend terminates in April 1986, being replaced by a medium term downtrend which appeared to last for nearly six months. The low point in October 1986 probably signals the end of this trend, but in the absence of data for 1987, this fact cannot be verified.

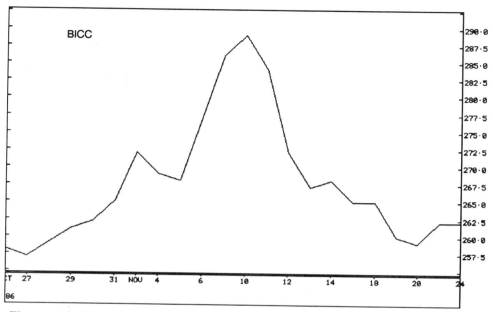

Figure 3.1. About one month of the BICC share price history.

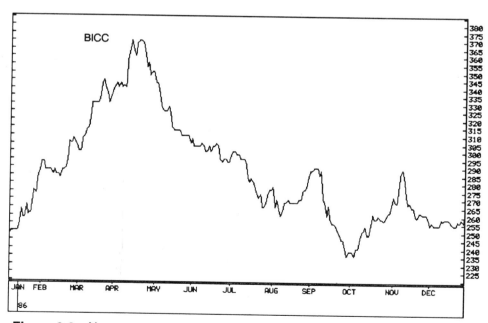

Figure 3.2. About one year of the BICC price history.

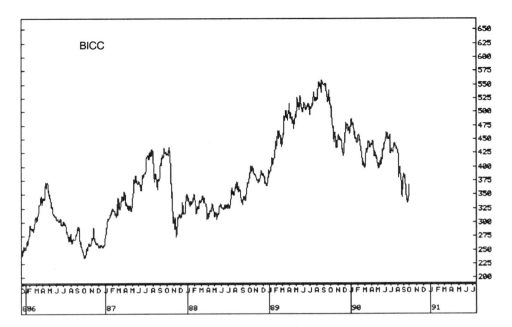

Figure 3.3. About five years of the BICC share price history.

Even longer term trends can be seen in Figure 3.3, where a plot of a longer period of the share price is shown. We can now see more clearly that the medium term downtrend we saw in Figure 3.2 had terminated in October 1986, being replaced by a new short term uptrend that lasted until the middle of November 1986. Now there are long term trends visible which last for over one year, for example the trend which began at the end of 1987 and peaked in late 1989. Still present of course in this chart are the medium and short term trends, and the day to day random movement which accounts for the fuzziness of the chart. Note the increasing importance of short term trends in the BICC share price from the beginning of 1990.

Besides the obvious point that as we open out to more and more of the share price history we can see trends of longer and longer persistence, we should also see that the rises and falls in price which are caused by these trends become large as the length of trend becomes greater. Thus short term trends in the BICC share price seem to generate rises and falls of approximately 50p, medium term trends seem to generate rises and falls of about 150p, and long term trends rises and falls of over 250p. In case these are not immediately obvious, look more closely at the short term trends in 1990, the medium term uptrend and downtrend in 1986 and the long term trend from the beginning of 1988 to late 1989. Many other short term trends and quite a few medium term trends should be visible on closer inspection.

Besides the absolute price range of a trend, another important property is the rate of change of the price for each type of trend. This is obtained by dividing the average price

Table 3.1. Rate of Change of the BICC Share Price for Various Trends.

Trend	Average Length of Time	Average Price Change	Rate of Change per Day
Short term	12 days	50p	4.16
Medium term	120 days	150p	1.25
Long term	500 days	225p	0.45

rise or fall by the average length of time for which the trend persists. To carry out such calculations requires several years of history of the share in question. The values will differ considerably from share to share, but as an example, approximate values for BICC are shown in Table 3.1.

Thus short term trends in the BICC price show rises of about 4p per day, medium term trends about 1p per day and long term trends about 0.5p per day. It is interesting that these rates of change are almost independent of the share price level. Because of that fact, the percentage change per day will vary depending upon where in the share price history the investor is standing when investments are being made. For example, in 1985 a change of 4p per day during the short term trend when the price level was about 200p represented a change of 2% per day, a rapid rate of increase in which dealing costs would be rapidly covered even if the investor entered the trend rather late. By the time the price was at the 500p level, the rate of increase was less than 1% per day, and such a rate of increase would make it difficult to recoup dealing costs if the investor entered the short term trend rather late and the trend was of less than average length.

Investors should always view shares in this light, determining the level of return which might be expected from the various trends, and unless there are grounds which suggest that a short term trend will be very profitable, should concentrate more on medium and long term trends as giving the greatest prospects for success.

The chart patterns which will be discussed in this book are caused by the interaction between trends of various lengths. Thus it will be possible to see short term head and shoulders patterns for example which take but a few weeks for completion, the same pattern which may take several months to complete, and very long term versions which make take several years over their formation.

Trends Tend to Continue

This may seem an obvious statement, but it is one of the basic facts upon which chartist techniques are based. A very good analogy can be found with the weather. The Meteorological Office has a record of correct forecasting of the weather about 75% of the time. A number of amateur weather forecasters who look at the behaviour of birds, or a string of seaweed can also achieve similar consistencies. What is not generally realised is that anyone can forecast the weather with at least 70% accuracy. All one has to do is state that tomorrow's weather will be the same as todays. The accuracy comes in because the weather does not swing wildly each day from rain to shine and back again. It stay in trends which usually last for quite a few days and occasionally for a few weeks.

Thus the amateur forecaster will be correct while this condition is maintained, but incorrect on the day the trend changes direction. Try keeping a record yourself for a few weeks and you will see how correct this method is.

Share prices behave in the same way. Although there is present random day to day movement, which will cause the price to rise one day and fall the next and rise the next and fall the next and so on, the trends we discussed above are quite the opposite. They make themselves visible above the random day to day movement because of the amount by which they make the price rise or fall. Whereas the random movement might be plus or minus 1p per day, the underlying trend might have a value of plus 1p each day while it lasts. The net result is of course additive, so that the total effect is for a standstill on days when the random movement is downwards, and a double rise of 2p on days when the random movement is upwards. These are not intended to be exact values, but simply to give an understanding on how the actual price movement observed may have arisen.

Further consideration of trends viewed in the same light as the weather brings one to the conclusion that each day, the most likely event is that the trend, be it short term, medium term or long term, will continue. The least likely event is that it will end. Unfortunately, from the investor's point of view, the most important facts that are required are the beginning and end of a trend, since these allow the investor to enter the market at the lowest price and exit at the highest price. The decision that the uptrend or downtrend will continue is naturally helpful, but is most helpful when an investor is already invested. If he is not invested, then the knowledge that the trend will continue has to be modified by a knowledge of for how long the trend has been in being before a decision to invest can be made. Probably more money has been lost by investors buying in far too late into an uptrend than has been lost by investors incorrectly anticipating the beginning of an uptrend.

Because of the importance of establishing the beginning and end of trends, chartist techniques have tended to focus primarily on this aspect. The features which enable an investor to determine, with various degrees of success the beginning or end of a trend, be it of a short term, medium term or long term nature are called reversal patterns. The direction of the trend before the pattern is formed reverses after the pattern has been formed. All of the indicators discussed in this book have been developed as aids to determining that a trend reversal has occurred. Of course, it is also useful to know that a trend should continue, and other patterns which can be used in this sense can be called continuation patterns. In these cases, the direction of the trend once the pattern has been completed is the same as the direction of the trend before the pattern was entered.

Drawing Trendlines

Earlier on when discussing the lengths of the trends in Figure 3.1, 3.2 and 3.3 their beginning and ends were more or less guessed at, although the clarity of the trends were such that the guesses were reasonably accurate. A much better idea of the direction of the trends can be obtained if trendlines are drawn.

For uptrends, trendlines are drawn by joining two troughs by a straight line. Since the line is straight, its direction remains constant, and this direction is the direction of the particular trend which is being studied. If the two troughs are a long way apart then the trend is long term. If the two troughs are close together, then the trend can be considered

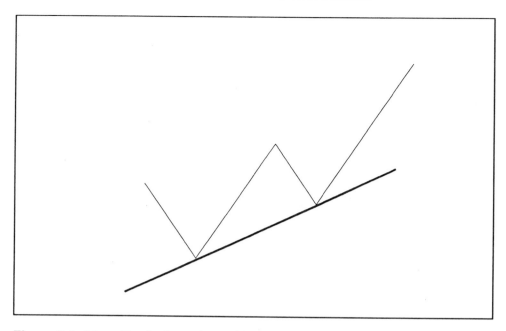

Figure 3.4. A trendline is drawn by making it pass through two successive troughs.

to be short term. Of course a trend which appeared to be a short term trend can turn into a long term trend. When this happens, not only the two original (and close together) troughs lie on the trendline, but subsequent troughs will also fall on the line.

In Figure 3.4 is shown how a trendline is constructed by joining two such troughs. The Figure intentionally gives no indication as to the distance apart in time of the two troughs, and gives no indication as to the vertical distance between them, i.e. the price rise occurring between the two points. Thus the trendline as shown may represent any length of trend from very short term to very long term.

This idea of trendlines can be transferred to a long term chart such as that of the BAA share price (Figure 3.5). A variety of short term, medium term and long term uptrends can be seen.

For downtrends, the trendlines are drawn by joining two peaks by a straight line. The same arguments apply as to uptrends, so that short term trends can turn into longer term trends, and third and subsequent peaks may also fall onto the trendline. In Figure 3.6 are shown a number of downtrends drawn on a chart of the Amstrad share price.

How trendlines isolate the trend

We now come to an important point about trendlines, and that is that a trendline is not the trend itself. As we have seen, a trendline is fairly easy to draw, but we have to be clear that such a trendline simply shows the direction and slope of the trend. The trend

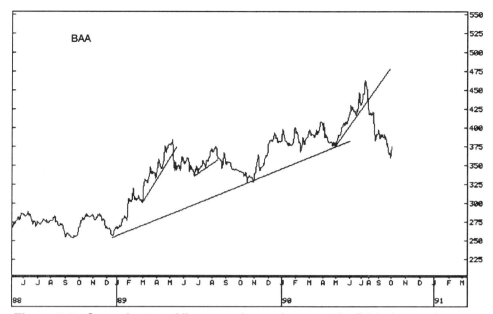

Figure 3.5. Several uptrend lines are shown drawn on the BAA share price.

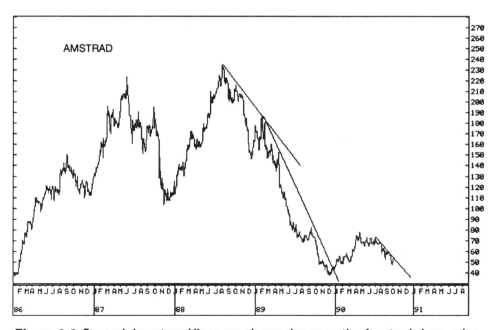

Figure 3.6. Several downtrend lines are shown drawn on the Amstrad share price.

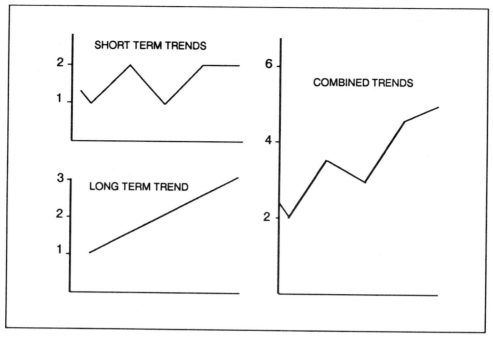

Figure 3.7. Short term trends can be combined additively with a long term trend to give the final result shown on the right.

itself is certainly not the line drawn by connecting successive peaks or successive troughs, but lies at a position higher than the troughs and lower than the peaks.

This comes about because all trends which are occurring at the same time are additive. It is worth spending some time on this concept because of its importance.

As an example, we can start from the position of having some shorter term trends in existence at the same time as a longer term trend. The short term trends are shown in the upper part of Figure 3.7. There are four successive ones, the first one rising for a few days, the next one falling for a few days, the third one rising again for a few days and the final one being a sideways movement. During the length of time for which these three short term trends are occurring, we can see what the effect will be of having a longer term trend present which is maintained for the whole time period in question. This trend can be an uptrend or a downtrend, and for this example is taken to be an uptrend. This longer term uptrend is shown in the middle part of Figure 3.7. Since the effect of all trends which are present at any one time is additive, the actual price movement that we see is obtained by adding these the shorter term and longer term trends together. You can easily do this for yourself since numerical values have been put on the left hand scale in the Figure. This net result is shown in the lower part of Figure 3.7.

If we now draw a trendline on this net result using the same procedure as for the BICC charts, as has been done in Figure 3.8, we can see that the drawn trendline has exactly

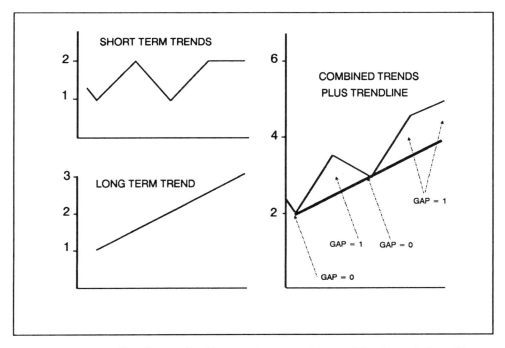

Figure 3.8. A trendline (heavy line) is now drawn on the combined trends from Figure 3.7. This has exactly the same slope as the original long term trend, thus the trend-line has isolated the long term trend. Note that the short term trends can be re-covered by plotting the gaps between the actual data and the superimposed trendline.

the same upward slope as the original longer term trend we started from in Figure 3.7. In other words, this simple method of drawing a trendline has isolated the direction and duration of the longer term trend for us. Note the important fact that the numerical values that we read off from the vertical scale for the trendline are not the same as those for the original trend. Thus our original contention that the trendline is not quite the same thing as the trend itself is justified.

Exactly the same approach can be used to isolate downtrends from combinations of shorter and longer term downtrends and even to isolate uptrends from combinations of short term downtrends and longer term uptrends and downtrends from combinations of short term uptrends and longer term downtrends.

Since the most important features of a trend are its direction and its time of persistence, the fact that both of these pieces of information are so easily obtained by drawing a trendline outweighs the fact that, numerically, trends and trendlines are somewhat different.

The more mathematically minded reader who has been trying the exercise of adding trends together where the successive short term trends are not of equal magnitude and

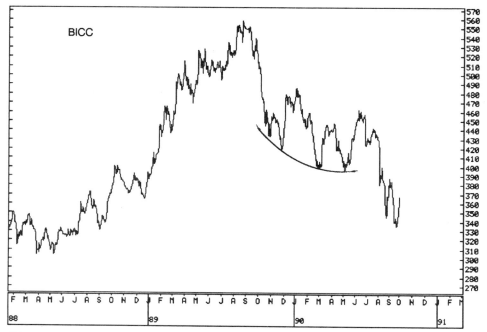

Figure 3.9. A curved trendline can be drawn on the BICC share price chart from the the latter half of 1989 to the middle of 1990.

timescale will find that the trendline drawn from such a starting point will not have the same direction and slope as the original longer term trend. Thus implicit in the drawing of trendlines is that the trends of shorter duration than the trend represented by the trendline being drawn are symmetrical, i.e. their upward moving legs last for exactly the same duration as the downward moving legs, and the movement covers the same price range. If trends are considered to be cyclical in nature, then both of these requirements fall into place, since any particular trend will rise for exactly the same length of time that it will fall, the sequence being repeated until the trend terminates. The advantage of viewing trends as being cyclical in nature is fundamental to the technique of channel analysis, which is discussed in the chapter 13.

So far we have been drawing trendlines as straight lines on the chart, looking for troughs or peaks which fall on such lines. Since we have just observed that trends are cyclical in nature, then any trendlines which are straight lines represent trends whose cycles occur over very long time scales. Any trends whose cycles repeat at much smaller intervals will not be straight lines but curves. Thus it is perfectly proper to draw curving trendlines as well as straight ones. As an example of this, a curved trendline is drawn on the BICC price chart shown in Figure 3.9.

The curved line in Figure 3.9 begins as a downtrend line. There is of course a difficulty with curved trendlines if we take the analogy with straight trendlines too far. This difficulty arises at the point where a curved downtrend becomes horizontal before rising

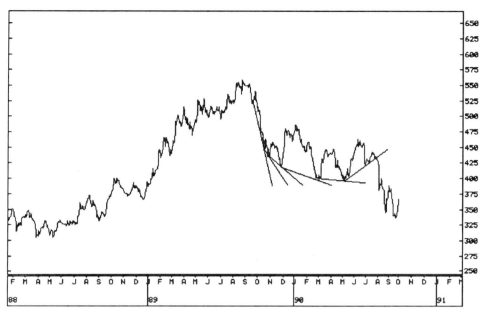

Figure 3.10. The curved trend shown in Figure 3.9 can also be highlghted by drawing a series of straight trendlines. These are called fanlines for obvious reasons.

again. We have distinguished straight uptrend lines from downtrend lines by virtue of
the fact that the downtrend line connects peaks while uptrend lines connect troughs.
Where a curved downtrend becomes horizontal before rising as an uptrend, logic would
dictate that we discontinue the curved downtrend line joining peaks and continue a new
line with the same rate of curvature which now joins the troughs. This is a case where we
should ignore logic, since it makes much more sense to continue the same downtrend
line onwards as an uptrend line, provided we still have new peaks falling on this line.
Taking this logic further, it is equally sensible to draw a curved downtrend line where
troughs are connected and continue this type of line onwards as an uptrend line.

This approach shows that the drawing of straight trendlines is not following logic but
is simply following a convention whereby downtrends connect peaks and uptrends
connect troughs. We shall not rock the boat but will continue to use this same convention
for straight lines while adopting the more flexible method of dealing with curved trends.

Displaying curved trends as a series of straight lines

Many chartists avoid wherever possible the drawing of curved lines, and use a different
approach to the highlighting of curved trends which uses the concept of fanlines. This is
shown in Figure 3.10 for the BICC share price. An uptrend line is drawn from a major
low point to the next trough. When a subsequent trough is formed, a second trendline is
drawn from the same starting point as the first trendline to this new trough. With each
succeeding trough which fails to fall onto the initial trendline, a new trendline is drawn,

but starting from the same initial point. Eventually the trendlines form an obvious fan shape emanating from this starting point.

What these fan lines are doing is showing that the underlying long term uptrend is flattening out, eventually to turn over and become a downtrend. The investor can stay with the share while these lines decrease in slope for as long as his nerve holds out. The unmistakable message is that the end of the uptrend is rapidly approaching, and that it is time to part company from that share.

The same situation applies to downtrends that are approaching termination, but of course in this case the fan lines will be drawn from a major peak and connected to successive peaks that fail to reach as high as the previous trendline.

CHAPTER 4

Theoretical Chart Patterns

Chart patterns are an essential part of technical analysis, but too many practitioners use them slavishly without real understanding. Chart patterns are successful in predicting the future direction of the market or of a share price, but are also frequently unsuccessful. Part of the failure can be attributed to an eagerness on the part of the investor which has him believing a particular pattern is being formed without waiting for further confirmation. Part of the failure can also be attributed to a failure of the pattern itself. It is this author's view that an understanding of the reasons why patterns are formed and why patterns sometimes fail is essential if an investor is to maximise the returns from investment in shares. This understanding will also lead to a more patient approach. Nothing but consistent losses can follow an investor who is continually jumping the gun and entering the market before the change in direction of a trend is confirmed. An investor who grasps the fundamental processes which lead to the formation of chart patterns will allow the market itself to dictate the correct timing for an investment decision. Such an investor will inevitably come out ahead of his less patient colleague.

In later chapters in this book, chart patterns are put into two categories, those which we can call reversal patterns and those which we can call continuation patterns. A reversal pattern is one where the direction of the trend at the point where it leaves the pattern is the reverse of the direction of the trend when it enters the pattern. Thus an uptrend becomes converted into a downtrend, or a downtrend becomes converted into an uptrend. A continuation pattern is one where the direction of the trend when it leaves the pattern is the same as the direction of the trend when it enters the pattern. Thus an uptrend passes through the pattern and still remains as an uptrend, and similarly for a downtrend.

Cyclical movement

All of the patterns which will be discussed can take place on a small, medium or large scale, i.e. can complete the formation in a matter of days, weeks or years. This is more easily understandable when it is considered that the patterns are formed from various combinations of cyclical movements in the market. Before taking this question of cycles any further it is necessary to have a clear idea of what is meant by a cyclical price movement. Such a movement is shown in Figure 4.1. The shape of this repetitive movement is probably better recognised by using the term 'sine wave'. Any sine wave is complete defined by three quantities, the wavelength, the amplitude and the phase. For the purposes of this book, it is not necessary to delve into any mathematics, but simply

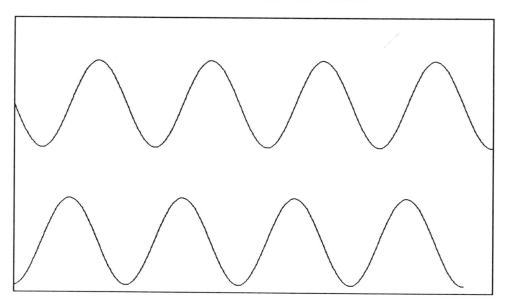

Figure 4.1. These two sine waves have identical amplitudes (trough to peak vertical distances) and identical wavelengths (peak to peak horizontal distances). Because their peaks do not occur at exactly the same points in time their phases are different.

to define what is meant by these three quantities defining the sine wave. By doing this we also define the cycles which are occurring in share price movement.

The wavelength of the sine wave is simply the distance from one point in the wave to the next similar point, i.e. the distance between two successive peaks, or the distance between two successive troughs. For share prices this wavelength will be in days for very short wavelength cycles, weeks for medium wavelength cycles and years for long wavelength cycles. The amplitude of the sine wave is the vertical distance moved, i.e. the vertical distance between a trough and the next or previous peak. This will be measured in points for an index such as the FTSE100, and in pence or pounds for a share price. The third quantity that specifies a sine wave is the phase. This simply means the distance between some arbitrary starting point and the first trough or peak in the wave. Thus the two sine waves shown in Figure 4.1 look identical, and are identical as far as amplitude and wavelength are concerned. They have different phases because the peaks in the upper sine wave occur at a different point in time from those in the lower sine wave. By shifting the phase in the lower sine wave, i.e. moving the whole sine wave to the right, a position can be reached in which the two waves can be exactly superimposed. When this happens the two waves are identical in every respect, wavelength, amplitude and phase. As far as the stock market is concerned, we shall not apply exact values to the phase of a sine wave. It is sufficient to recognise when two waves are exactly in phase at some particular time of interest (two peaks coincide), when they are exactly out of phase at some particular time (a peak of one coincides with a trough of the other) and when they are partly out of phase (neither two peaks nor a peak and a trough coincide). Patterns in share price movement will become much more meaningful with these fairly simple concepts of phase. Note the important property of sine waves in that they are perfectly symmetrical. For this reason patterns which are composed of only one cycle or perhaps the combination of two cycles are usually symmetrical about a vertical centre line. Where three cycles are involved the patterns may be symmetrical or otherwise about a vertical centre line.

The proper meaning of the term 'cycle' as applied to a sine wave is the part of the wave from any starting point on the wave to the next similar point, e.g. from one trough to the next, from one peak to the next or from a point halfway up a left hand rising side to the next point halfway up a left hand rising side. This is one cycle of the sine wave. However, in technical analysis, the term has become misused to apply to the whole sine wave. Thus the term '20 day cycles' means a sine wave with a wavelength of 20 days, but of unspecified amplitude (and phase).

At this point, it is useful to clarify the trends which were discussed in the last chapter in terms of sine waves or cycles. An uptrend is the part of the cyclical movement from a trough to the succeeding peak, while a downtrend is the part of the cyclical movement from a peak to the next trough. Thus an uptrend is one half of a complete cycle using the correct meaning of the term 'cycle' and a downtrend is also one half of a complete cycle. It should now be obvious that the length of an uptrend or a downtrend is one half of the wavelength of the cyclical movement concerned. Thus cycles of wavelength 20 days from peak to peak will give uptrends of 10 days and downtrends of 10 days.

Before moving on to the way in which various patterns are produced by combinations of cycles, it is necessary to point out that in all of these theoretical shapes, cycles of much shorter wavelength than the timescale of the pattern itself as well as day to day random price movements are omitted for the purposes of clarity. Naturally in the real world of the charts that will be analysed throughout this book, these other movements all coexist, but since they have no effect on the underlying longer term patterns being observed they can be ignored for the purposes of analysis.

Trend Reversal patterns

(a) Single top

(1) Rounded top

This is the simplest possible pattern, since, as mentioned above, if cycles of very much shorter wavelength and random movements are ignored, all that is left is a curved trend which is the top part of a cyclical waveform of the appropriate wavelength. Only one such cyclical waveform is involved, and there is no interaction with any other waveform of say half, one quarter or one eighth of the dominant waveform. The derivation of a rounded top formation from one waveform is shown in Figure 4.2. The rounded top pattern should be symmetrical for a limited distance either side of a vertical line drawn through the peak price, and this line of symmetry is shown in Figure 4.2. The cleaner is the rounded top, i.e. the freer from combination with other cyclical movements, the

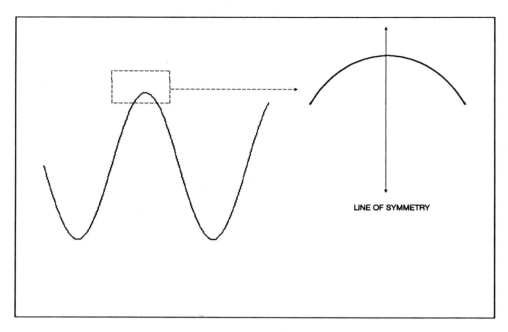

Figure 4.2. How a rounded top formation is simply the top of a long wavelength cycle.

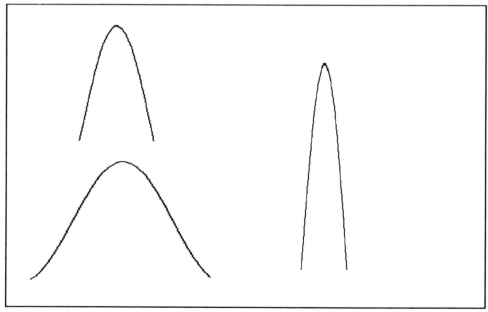

Figure 4.3. How a sharp top formation on the right) is simply the coincidence of the peaks of two different cycles (on the left). This coincidence accentuates the rate of rise and fall.

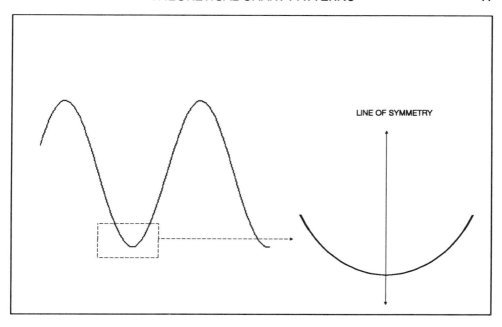

LINE OF SYMMETRY

Figure 4.4. How a rounded bottom formation is simply the bottom of a long wavelength cycle.

further does the symmetry extend either side of the line of symmetry. Rounded tops can take perhaps a year for their complete formation or may only take a few weeks, depending upon the nature of the dominant cycle causing the formation.

(2) Sharp top

The rounded top reflects the fact that sentiment about the share price is taking a long time to unravel, so that there is a long battle between the buyers and the sellers. On the other hand a sharp top reflects a rapid change in sentiment for the worse. In cyclic terms, there is a short term cycle superimposed on a longer term cycle such that the two peaks are more or less coincident in time. The way in which a sharp top is formed is shown in Figure 4.3.

(b) Single bottom

(1) Rounded bottom

All of the comments about a rounded top apply to a rounded bottom, with the exception that a rounded bottom is the bottom part of a cyclical waveform. An example of a rounded bottom with a line of symmetry is shown in Figure 4.4.

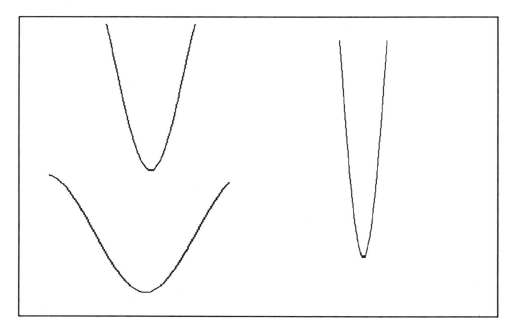

Figure 4.5. How a sharp bottom formation on the right) is simply the coincidence of the troughs of two different cycles (on the left). This coincidence acentuates the rate of fall and rise.

(2) Sharp bottom

This is formed in the same way as the sharp top, with a short term cycle superimposed on a longer term cycle. The troughs in both occur more or less at the same point in time. An example of a sharp bottom is shown in Figure 4.5.

(c) Double top

Now we move on to a pattern which is caused by the combination of two cycles. The dominant cycle is the one which causes the pattern to be a reversal pattern, i.e. the dominant cycle is passing through its peak. In the absence of another cycle we would simply have a rounded top formation.

In addition to the dominant cycle we have another one present which is reaching its trough as the dominant cycle reaches its peak. This second cycle usually has a wavelength of about half of that of the dominant cycle. Thus while the dominant cycle is passing through its maximum there is time for two complete waveforms of the second cycle to be formed. The way a double top is formed from these two cycles is shown in Figure 4.6 along with the line of symmetry.

The double top formation will start to lose its symmetry if the trough of the second cycle is not exactly coincident.

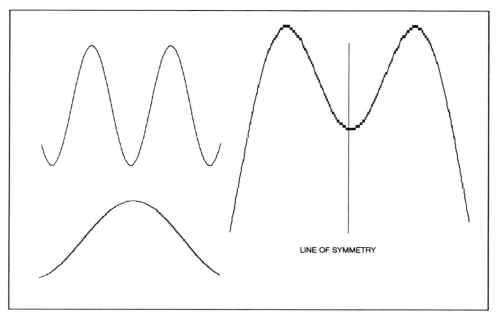

Figure 4.6. How a double top pattern is formed by the coincidence of the trough of one cycle with the peak of a longer term cycle.

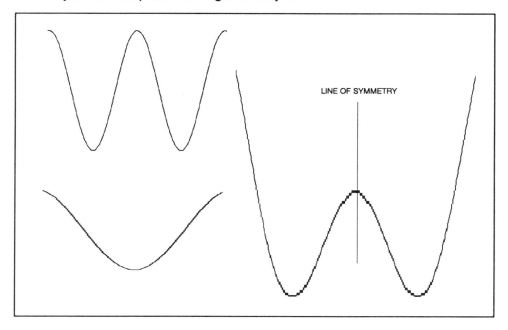

Figure 4.7. How a double bottom pattern is formed by the coincidence of the peak of one cycle with the trough of a longer term cycle.

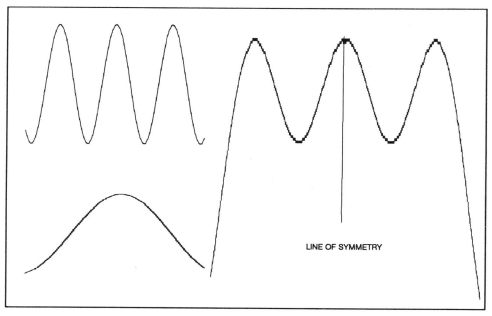

LINE OF SYMMETRY

Figure 4.8. Triple tops are formed by the same process as double tops, but the subordinate cycle (upper) is of much shorter wavelength than the dominant cycle (lower).

(d) Double bottom

All of the comments about a double top apply equally well to a double bottom, with the exception that the dominant cycle is passing through its trough while the second cycle is passing through its peak. The wavelength of the second cycle is usually about half of that of the dminant cycle. A symmetrical double bottom formation is shown in Figure 4.7.

(e) Triple top

A triple top is formed by the combination of two cycles, the second cycle being much more different in wavelength from the dominant cycle than is the case with double tops. This means that while the dominant cycle is passing through its maximum there is time for three complete waveforms of the second cycle to be formed. A completely symmetrical triple top is shown in Figure 4.8. Because there are two ways in which the formation can be asymmetric, a completely symmetric triple top formation is not as common as the asymmetric versions. The asymmetry can take the form of a different distance between the first and second tops compared with the second and third tops, or it can take the form of different heights for each of the three tops or different levels for the two troughs between the three tops. Such asymmetric triple tops are shown in Figure 4.9.

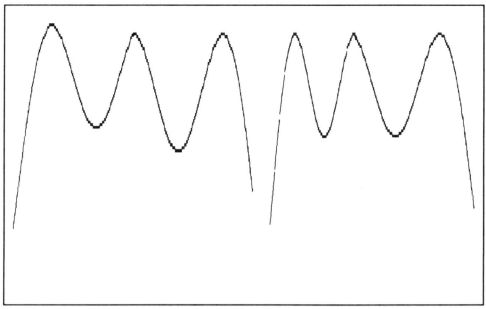

Figure 4.9. Asymmetric triple tops. The left hand peaks and troughs are not at the same levels. The right hand peaks are unevenly spaced in time.

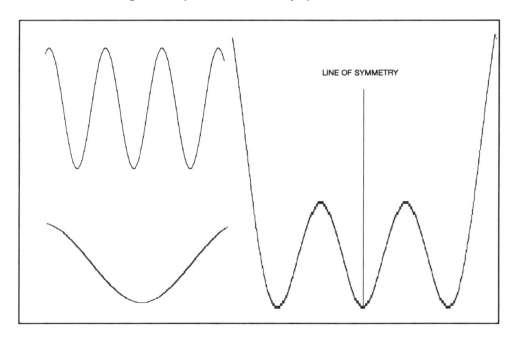

Figure 4.10. Triple bottoms are formed by the same process as double bottoms, but the subordinate cycle (upper) is of much shorter wavelength than the dominant cycle (lower).

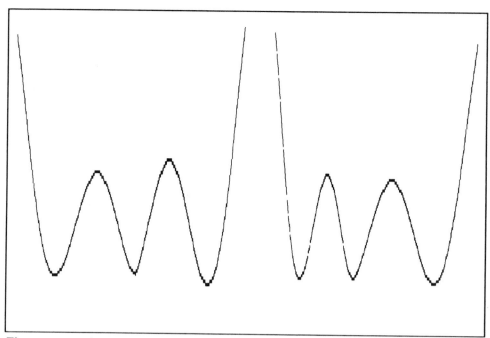

Figure 4.11. Asymmetric triple bottoms. The left hand peaks and troughs are not at the same levels. The right hand peaks are unevenly spaced in time.

(d) Triple bottom

As with the relationship between the previous top and bottom formations the same comments about symmetry and asymmetry apply to triple bottoms. Triple bottoms are caused by the dominant cycle passing through its minimum while interacting with a second cycle of considerably shorter wavelength. Examples of symmetric and asymmetric triple bottoms are shown in Figure 4.10 and 4.11.

(e) Head and shoulders

These are formed by a similar combination of cycles to a triple top. The amplitude of the secondary cycle is at its maximum at the point where the middle of the three cycles occurs, and therefore causes the middle peak to be higher than either of the outside peaks. The middle peak is therefore the 'head' and the outside peaks the 'shoulders' of the pattern. The 'neckline' of the pattern is the horizontal line which joins the two troughs, one either side of the head. An example of a symmetrical head and shoulders pattern is shown in Figure 4.12. The line of symmetry is the vertical passing through the centre of the head.

More often than not, the pattern is not quite symmetrical. The usual asymmetry is that the neckline is not quite horizontal, but either slopes upward or downward. Occasionally the neckline is horizontal but one shoulder is higher than the other. Rarer examples of asymmetry show a double head or a double shoulder.

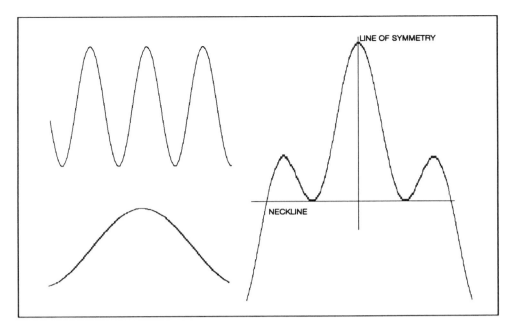

Figure 4.12. A head and shoulders is formed by a combination of a long term cycle and a short term cycle. The head is higher than the shoulders because a short term peak coincides with the maximum of the long term peak.

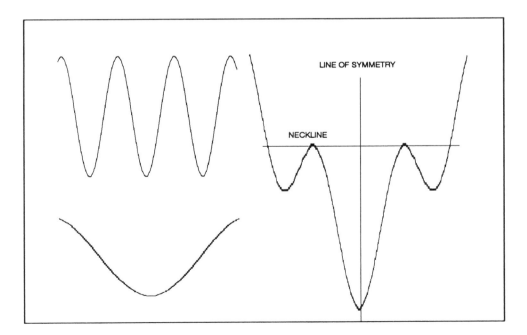

Figure 4.13. An inverted head and shoulders is formed by a combination of a long term cycle and a short term cycle. The inverted head is lower than the shoulders because a short term trough coincides with the minimum of the long term peak.

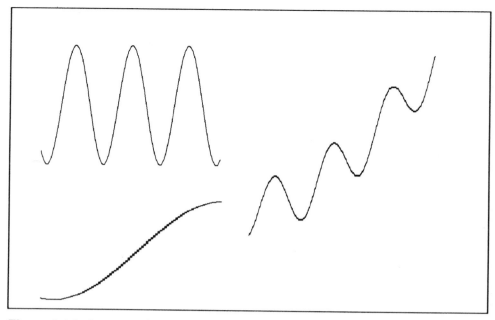

Figure 4.14. An uptrend is formed by a combination of a long term cycle and a short term cycle. The dominant longer term cycle on on its way up to its maximum.

(d) Inverted head and shoulders

These are formed by a similar combination of cycles to a triple bottom, but the middle bottom falls to a lower level than the bottom on either side. Since the pattern is inverted, it is still in order to refer to the neckline and shoulders. The shoulders of an inverted head and shoulders are of course the low points reached by the bottoms at each side of the centre one, while the neckline is the line joining the peaks which lie between the inverted head and the inverted shoulders. A perfectly symmetrical inverted head and shoulders pattern is shown in Figure 4.13.

Trend Continuation Patterns

The reversal patterns discussed above are reversal patterns simply because of the status of the dominant cycle, which is either topping out or bottoming out. On the other hand the trend continuation patterns are ones in which the dominant cycle is not at a top or bottom but is either rising towards the peak or falling towards the trough, but still with some way to go.

(e) Uptrend

This is a combination of a dominant cycle in a rising mode with a cycle of shorter wavelength superimposed. The troughs of the uptrend fall either on a straight line if the dominant cycle has a particularly long wavelength, or they can fall on a curve if the

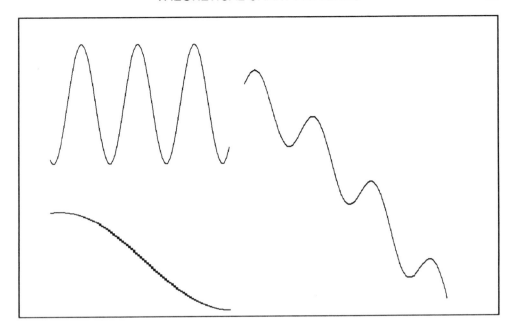

Figure 4.15. An downtrend is formed by a combination of a long term cycle and a short term cycle. The dominant longer term cycle on on its way down to its minimum.

dominant cycle has a more obvious curve. If the curve is of increasing slope then the dominant trend has some way to go to its peak, whereas with a decreasing slope the dominant trend is approaching its peak. An example of a straight line uptrend is shown in Figure 4.14.

(f) Downtrend

Again, this is a combination of a dominant cycle which is in a falling mode with a cycle of shorter wavelength superimposed. The peaks of the downtrend can fall on a straight line if the dominant cycle is of particularly long wavelength, or they can fall on a curve if the dominant cycle is not of particularly long wavelength. If the down slope is increasing in curvature then the downtrend has some way to go, whereas if the down slope is decreasing in curvature the downtrend is approaching its trough. An example of a straight downtrend is shown in Figure 4.15.

(g) Upchannels

These are a particular form of uptrend. In this case the secondary cycles are of such regularity that lines joining the troughs and lines joining the peaks can be drawn parallel to each other in the case of straight channels or concentric in the case of curved channels.

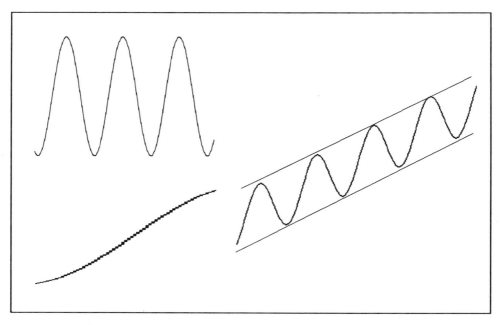

Figure 4.16 An upchannel (right) is formed by a combination of a very long term cycle (lower left) and a short term cycle (upper left). The dominant longer term cycle on on its way up to its maximum. Because of its long wavelength, the upward leg is almost a straight line.

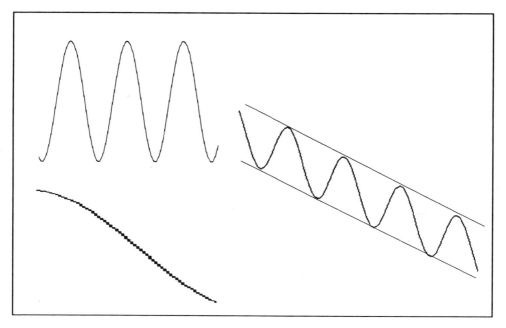

Figure 4.17. An downchannel (right) is formed by a combination of a very long term cycle (lower left) and a short term cycle (upper left). The dominant longer term cycle on on its way down to its minimum. Because of its long wavelength, the downward leg is almost a straight line.

The same comments about straight and curved uptrends apply to upchannels. An example of a straight upchannel is shown in Figure 4.16.

(h) Downchannels

These are a specific form of downtrend again with the secondary cycles of such regular amplitude than the lines joining the peaks and troughs are parallel in the case of straight channels and concentric in the case of curved channels. The same comments about straight and curved downtrends apply to downchannels. An examples of a straight downchannel is shown in Figure 4.17.

Ambiguous patterns

The trend reversal and trend continuation patterns were so called because more often than not they correctly call the future direction of the trend. Therefore as the particular pattern is unfolding, the investor has a reasonable expectation for the future course of events. Ambiguous patterns are in a different category, since they sometimes act as continuation patterns and sometimes as reversal patterns. Although in the next chapter we urge caution on the part of the investor, who should wait for confirmation of a pattern formation, it is doubly important that an investor should wait for the following ambiguous patterns to be resolved before making any investment decision.

(i) Support lines

In a sense, a support line is similar to a perfect triple bottom. It is formed by the combination of a long wavelength cycle that is passing through a horizontal phase and a cycle of much shorter wavelength. This cycle is of much shorter wavelength relative to the dominant cycle than is the case with the triple bottom.

In the case of support lines, the price falls to a level before bouncing back upwards, and this level is one that has seen similar behaviour previously. A support level can be revisited by the share price at very long time intervals. A horizontal line can be drawn at this support level. Buyers are attracted as the support level is reached, thus causing the price to rise. Often the support level is at a 'round' level such as a multiple of 100p. Once a support level has been breached by a fall in price below it, the level then often becomes a resistance level. An example of a support line is shown in Figure 4.18.

(j) Resistance lines

This is formed similarly to a support line by a combination of a long term cycle passing through its horizontal phase plus a cycle of shorter wavelength. When the price rises to this level, it then rebounds downwards. The level is one which has seen similar behaviour in the past, and as with support lines, they may be revisited a quite widely separated time intervals. Again, they frequently occur at rounded price levels such as multiples of 10p or 100p. An example is shown in Figure 4.19. Once breached by a rise in price above the resistance level, such resistance lines can often become future support lines.

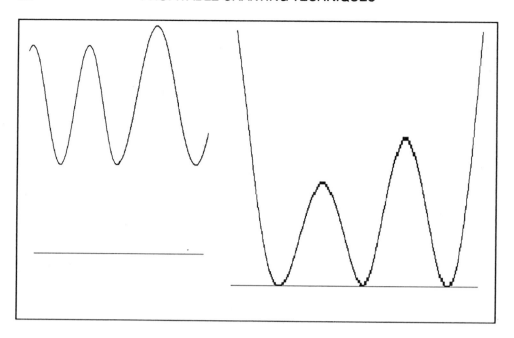

Figure 4.18. Support lines are formed by a similar process as triple bottoms. but the subordinate cycle (upper) is of much shorter wavelength than the dominant cycle (lower) and may be of irregular amplitude. The dominant cycle is almost horizontal.

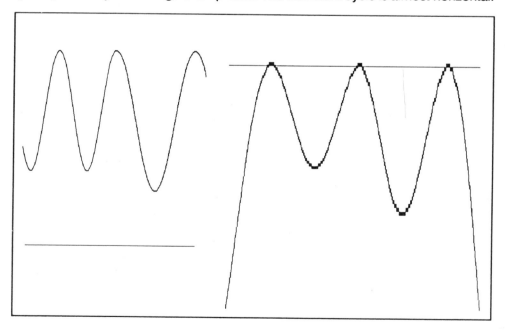

Figure 4.19. Resistance lines are formed by a similar process as triple tops. but the subordinate cycle (upper) is of much shorter wavelength than the dominant cycle (lower) and may be of irregular amplitude. The dominant cycle is at a horizontal phase.

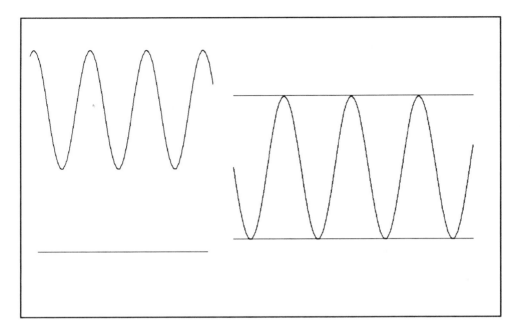

Figure 4.20. Rectangles are formed by a similar process to upchannels and down-channels, but the dominant cycle is passing through a horizontal phase.

(k) Rectangles

A rectangle is a specific form of a channel, which rather than rising or falling as an upchannel or downchannel, is moving horizontally. It is therefore formed by a combination of a long term cycle which is moving horizontally, plus an extremely regular short term cycle with constant amplitude. It is a congested area which is bounded on the upper side by a resistance line and on the lower side by a support line. The price therefore oscillates between these two levels. Obviously there comes a time when the price breaks out on either the upper or lower side, but which of these two will occur is not predictable. An example of a rectangle is shown in Figure 4.20.

(l) Triangles

Triangles can take two main forms. The first is where the price movement is becoming more pronounced as time unfolds. These are called expanding triangles, which are fairly rare in occurrence. The other form is where the price movement is decreasing as time unfolds, so that the triangle is contracting. These are much more common, and fall into various categories such as ascending right angled, descending right angled, isosceles (two sides equal in length) and scalene (all sides unequal in length). The latter is also called a wedge.

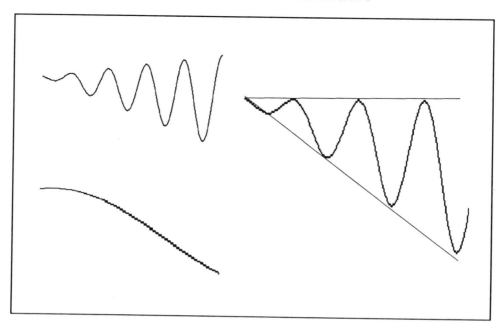

Figure 4.21. Expanding triangles are formed by a combination of a short term cycle with an increasing amplitude and a long term cycle that may be rising, as above, falling or passing through a horizontal phase.

(1) Expanding triangle

Whereas the head and shoulders and inverted head and shoulders patterns were characterised by the central of three complete waveforms of the secondary cycles being of greater amplitude than the outside ones, the expanding triangle has the secondary cycles increasing in amplitude as the price unfolds. At some point the price has to break out, either on the upside or the downside. An example of an expanding triangle is shown in Figure 4.21.

(2) Ascending triangle

This formation is a right-angled triangle with the upper side horizontal. It is caused by the combination of a dominant cycle which is in a rising phase and a shorter wavelength cycle whose amplitude is decreasing with time. Thus the usual resolution of the triangle is that the rise will continue, since the dominant cycle is in a rising mode. However, as with all contracting triangle formations, if the price exits through the apex the significance is lost. An example is shown in Figure 4.22.

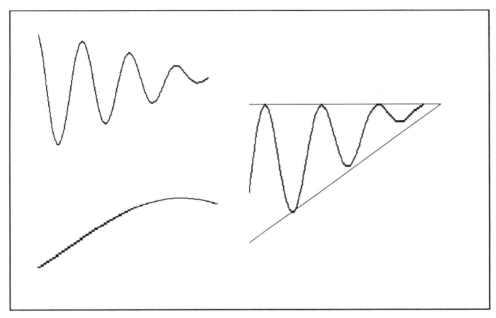

Figure 4.22. Ascending triangles are formed by a combination of a short term cycle with a decreasing amplitude and a long term cycle that is rising.

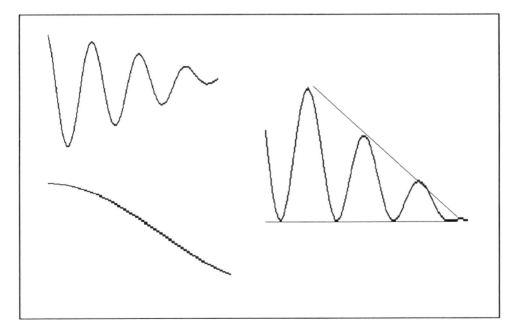

Figure 4.23. Descending triangles are formed by a combination of a short term cycle with a decreasing amplitude and a long term cycle that is falling.

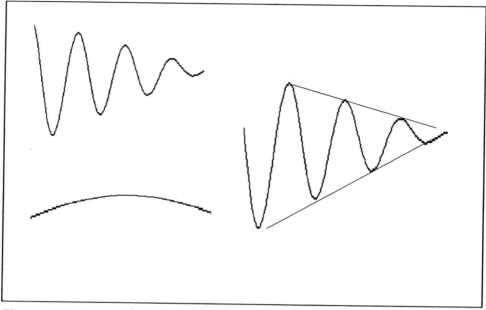

Figure 4.24. Isosceles triangles are formed by a combination of a short term cycle with a decreasing amplitude and a long term cycle that is almost horizontal.

(3) Descending triangle

This formation is caused by the same combination of cycles as in the ascending triangle, the difference being that the dominant cycle is in a falling phase. It is this direction of the dominant cycle that leads to the usual resolution of the pattern into a continuing fall. The usual resolution of the triangle does not follow if the price exits through the apex. An example is shown in Figure 4.23.

(4) Isosceles triangle

This formation is caused by the same combination of cycles as the right angled triangles, but with the important difference that the dominant cycle is passing through a horizontal phase, neither rising nor falling. Thus the triangle is essentially symmetrical about a horizontal line through its apex. Whether the triangle is a reversal or continuation pattern depends upon the status of an even longer term cycle than the triangle dominant cycle, but the balance seems to lie slightly on the side of continuation. An exit through the apex takes the meaning out of the triangle. An example is shown in Figure 4.24.

(5) Scalene triangle or wedge

It is possible to have triangles which are wedge shaped, i.e. which are neither right-angled nor symmetrical in the sense that the isosceles triangle is. The usual

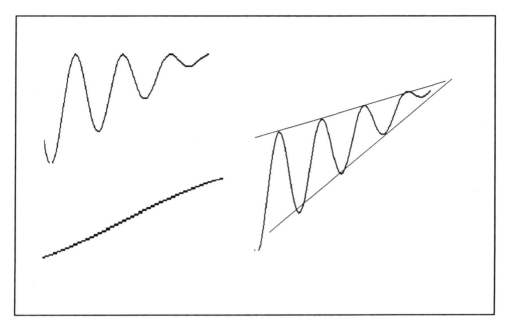

Figure 4.25. Wedges are formed by a combination of a descending or ascending triangle and and a long term cycle that is falling or rising.

resolution of a wedge is that the price reverses the direction of its trend. An example of a wedge is shown in Figure 4.25.

(m) Flags

Flags are specific varieties of triangles, and occasionally channels, which persist for only a short period of time. In general chartists take this period to be a maximum of three weeks. The flag is halfway up or down a steep trend, and as such represent a breathing point before the trend continues in its previous direction. All the various types of triangles noted above are possible as these mini-versions, and for channels the slope for the short duration in which they persist can be upward or downward sloping. Examples of flags are shown in Figure 4.26.

(n) Earthquakes

This is a fairly rare pattern which appears to be ignored on other texts on technical analysis or charting techniques. In a real life earthquake a portion of land can slip down below the level of the surrounding land, the edges of the fall being vertical. A similar occurrence can occur in share prices, from the point of view that a sudden vertical fall in price can be matched later by an equally vertical rise. When the vertical rise will occur is not predictable, and the rapidity of the rise is such that it is difficult for the investor to climb aboard the rise at a sensible price level. The interesting facet of the earthquake

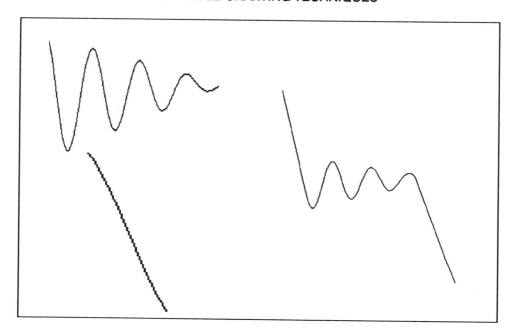

Figure 4.26. Flags are formed by a combination of a very short term cycle of reducing amplitude and a rapidly rising or falling medium term cycle.

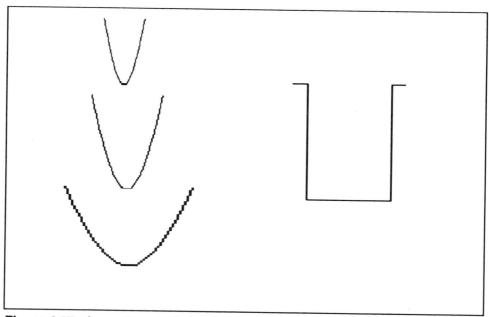

Figure 4.27. An earthquake is formed by a combination of cycles that are all falling to a trough simultaneously.

pattern that can be of great use to investors is that it seems to be an aberration in the longer term trend of the share price, in other words the price seems to continue after the vertical rise with the same trend that it had before the vertical fall. An example is shown in Figure 4.27.

CHAPTER 5

Confirmation of Patterns

The buying and selling of shares based purely on pattern formation is but one part of the overall concept of technical analysis. With practice it is possible to realise good returns from investment decisions based purely on the patterns which we discussed in the last chapter, and the next few chapters will concentrate on this aspect. Later chapters discuss the importance of indicators as aids to buying and selling decisions, and there is no doubt that the investor who uses all the tools at his disposal, pattern formation and indicators, will achieve more consistent results than the one who relies solely on patterns. That being said, it is still necessary to show how investment decisions can be based on pattern formation.

All successful investors knowingly or unknowingly use methods which are based on taking advantage of probability. Taking a very simplified view, investors who do not do this will have only a 50% chance of being correct in an investment decision. If dealing costs and the difference, i.e. spread of buying and selling prices for a share are taken into consideration then the odds move against the investor, perhaps as far as giving him only a 40% chance of success. The rationale behind using pattern formation for investment is that share prices passing through a recognised reversal pattern, such as those discussed in the last chapter, more often than not will show a change in the direction of the trend. Share prices passing through a continuation pattern will more often than not show a continuation in the direction of the trend. Where investors often go wrong is in translating the phrase "more often than not" into a very high probability, such as 90% or more, that the future course of the share price will continue as predicted. The probability is nothing like as high as that, and at a guess a value of 55% is nearer to the mark. This may not sound high enough to make profits, but over a large number of transactions the investor will inevitably make profits. Better profits will be made if the investor employs a good stop loss method, so that losing situations are terminated quickly, while winning situations are allowed to run. A good analogy for the value of small favourable percentages is with roulette, where the percentage in favour of the house due to the presence of a zero or double zero is quite small, but few people would question the statement that casinos make profits.

The investor should pay much more attention to reversal patterns than continuation patterns for the simple reason that recognition that a share is passing through a continuation pattern usually requires no further action from the investor. On the other hand a reversal formation can signal to the investor that a buying opportunity is becoming imminent. As we discuss later in this chapter, an investor should never be in the position that he relies on a topping pattern to tell him when to sell. For this reason this chapter

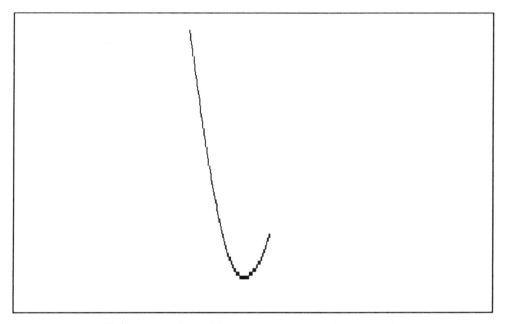

Figure 5.1. A falling share price which appears to have bottomed out.

discusses reversal patterns at bottoms, and at what stage in their development that a buying decision can be made with the greatest chance of success. For the investor in shares, reversal patterns at tops are considered more in the light of an indication to the investor that the share should be put on the back burner for a while. Investors in options fall into a totally different category, since the knowledge that a share may be in a falling trend is just as valuable that a share may now be in a rising trend.

In order to achieve the small favourable percentage which is available from correct recognition of a pattern, it is vital to wait for confirmation that a pattern is complete. It is only then that the investor can move the balance of probability in his favour. The necessity of doing this is readily illustrated by an example of a falling share price which has apparently bottomed out, as shown in Figure 5.1. The investor would therefore be contemplating buying the share in question.

The first thought is that this is a rounded bottom formation, since the shape traced by the price movement so far has passed through a fairly gentle minimum. More thought will lead to the conclusion that the pattern so far could also be the start of a double bottom, a triple bottom or even an inverted head and shoulders where the first trough is somewhat more rounded than usual. These possibilities are shown in Figure 5.2. If this is the case, not too much damage is done by buying at this early stage in the pattern formation, since these other possibilities are all trend reversal patterns, and therefore there is no advantage in continuing to hold off from the share for any length of time.

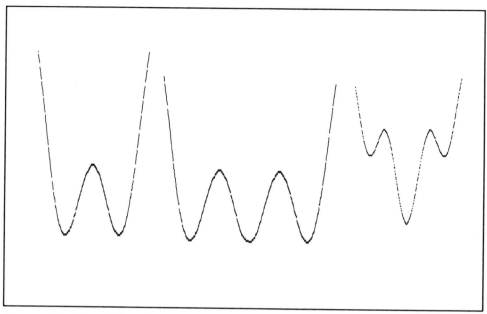

Figure 5.2. The falling share price may be entering a variety of bottoming formations.

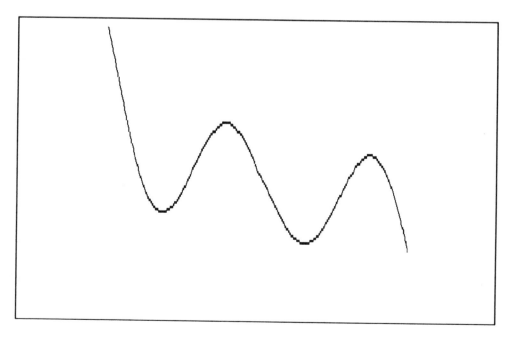

Figure 5.3. The falling share price may also be entering a variety of continuation patterns such as a downtrend.

This approach neglects some other possibilities, such as an downtrend or downchannel formation, as shown in Figure 5.3. It would be incorrect to buy at this juncture since these patterns are trend continuation patterns. Such premature buying would expose the investor to a loss, and it could well be years before the share price moves back above this original buying level.

The above comments leads to the conclusion that we need a set of rules to apply to enable us to know whether a pattern has been completed, i.e. the formation in Figure 5.1 does turn out to be a rounded bottom, or whether it is incomplete, i.e. the formation in Figure 5.1 is the first part of an new downtrend. The rules should be concerned with deciding how far up from the bottom of the first part of the formation shown in Figure 5.1. we should allow the share price to rise before buying. This can only be done by studying a large number of shares in order to decide how far shares rise from the bottom before the next downward wave in an downtrend commences. Once a rise exceeds this usual value, then we can say with much more confidence that the downtrend is not going to occur, and that we are embarked on a uptrend, and therefore it is correct to buy. If the price turns down before rising this distance, then we can wait for the next phase of the pattern to unfold before taking a decision. When we come to the chapters on indicators, it will be seen that most of the rules are already enshrined in the way in which indicators are calculated and used, which enforces the view expressed earlier that the best results are obtained from a combination of pattern formation and indicator techniques.

Of the possible bottoming patterns of single bottom, double bottom, triple bottom and inverted head and shoulders, the single bottom, be it of the rounded or sharp variety, is the most difficult to establish. The reason is that all of the other patterns give an intermediate rise followed by a fall before a further rise, and the level reached by the first rise can be used to designate a ceiling through which the price must rise before the share can be considered a buy. Another way of looking at things is that the level of the first rise is a resistance level, so that a rise through it is a good positive sign. The single rounded bottom has no such level, and therefore there is nothing to indicate that the share has passed into a bullish phase. Fortunately the single bottom is the least common of the bottoming formations. Because of this fact, and the difficulty associated with it of determining when its formation is complete, investors should not take action on a single bottom formation unless one or more indicators can confirm that the new trend of the share price is upwards. Never forget the golden rule that amongst the large number of shares which can be followed, there will nearly always be another share in which a more significant pattern can be found. If this is not the case, then do nothing until such an opportunity does arise. Never force an investment decision out of an indecisive chart pattern.

Having decided that we will not take action at the point reached by the share price in Figure 5.1, we can wait for it to unfold a bit further to the position shown in Figure 5.4. Now the share price has turned down again, giving us an important resistance level which the price failed to penetrate on this first attempt. Thus we take no action until the price rises above this level in the future. Naturally, as soon as the price starts to rise again from this current fall we start to take notice, because the price may now be setting out on the upward leg which will penetrate this resistance level. As well as the resistance level noted

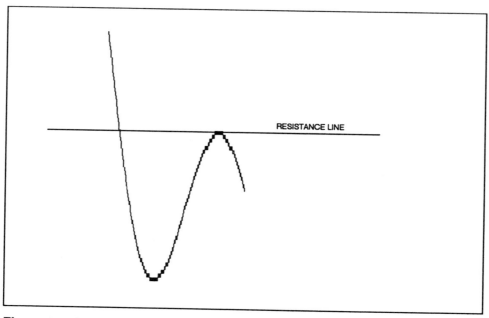

Figure 5.4. The share price has reached a resistance line and reversed direction.

for the intermediate rise, another important feature will be the position of the second trough which will have been formed once the price starts to rise back towards the resistance level. For the formation to be considered to be a double bottom the second trough should be within 3% of the price at the first trough.

There are now two possibilities, firstly that the price will not rise this far before falling again, and secondly, that the price will pass through the resistance level. These two possibilities are shown in Figure 5.5. If the first possibility occurs, then what we have happening is that the share price is still in a downtrend. This can be visualised by drawing a trendline through the two successive peaks. Quite obviously, since the second peak is lower than the first peak, then the trend is still downwards. If the price moves above the first peak, then the trend is upwards, since any subsequent peak that will be formed must be at a higher level than this first peak.

This move of the price above the resistance level, being a sign that an uptrend is now in being, is a signal to buy the share.

Another possibility which will preclude a buy even if the price rises through the resistance level is that the second trough which is formed is not within 3% of the price of the first trough, i.e. the formation does not pass the first test for a double bottom. This leads to two further possibilities, either the second trough is much higher than the first trough, or it is much lower. If the trough is higher, then it is permissible to draw a trendline through these two troughs, and this trendline will slope upwards. We are therefore in an uptrend, and so the investor can consider buying that share. If on the

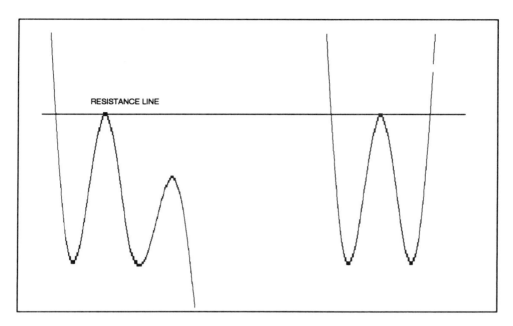

Figure 5.5. On rebounding from the second trough, the price may fail to rise to to the previous resistance line, i.e. may be now entering a downtrend. Alternatively, it may rise through the reistance line to form a double bottom.

other hand the second trough is lower then there are two further possibilities, either we are still in a downtrend or we are entering an inverted head and shoulders reversal pattern. The first two of these possibilities are shown in Figure 5.6.

Now supposing that that the share has passed the first test for a double bottom, i.e. the second trough is within 3% of the price of the first trough, then all depends upon whether or not the price continues to rise above the resistance level created by the first peak. If it does, all well and good because we have now complete a double bottom formation and the share price has now reversed direction to enter a new uptrend. This is now a signal to buy the share.

If on the other hand the price retreats again, then the possibility arises that we are seeing a triple bottom formation. The crucial determining factor for this is the position of the third trough. If it is within 3% of either of the two previous troughs, then we are on course for a triple bottom, and all that remains is for the share price to rise above the resistance level formed by the previous two peaks. This will be the signal to buy since the trend reversal pattern is now complete. If the share price does not rise through the resistance level then the direction of the trend is not resolved and the share should be left alone. These possibilities are shown in Figure 5.7.

If the third trough is not within 3% of the level of the previous two troughs, then the pattern is not a triple bottom. If this third trough is higher than the previous two, then it is possible than the trend direction has already been reversed, and we have what can be

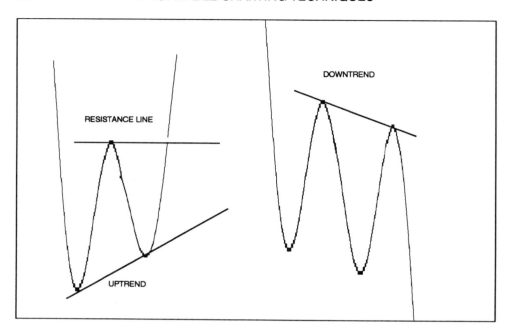

Figure 5.6. The second trough may be higher than the first, in which case the share may be entering an uptrend (left). Alternatively, if the second trough is lower than the first, the price may be entering a downtrend (right).

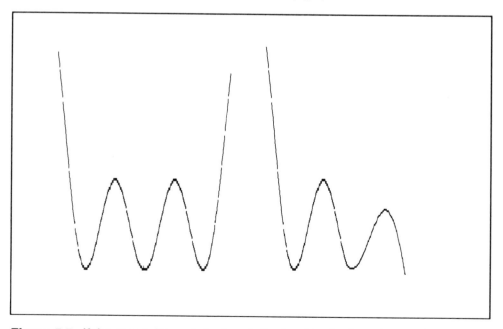

Figure 5.7. If the second trough is at a similar level to the first, then a triple bottom formation is a strong possibility (left). If this is not the case, the pattern is unresolved (right).

Table 5.1. Possible outcomes from a falling share price.

Position	Action	Possible formation
After first trough	price continues to rise	single bottom
	price forms a peak and then falls	double bottom
		triple bottom
		inverted head and shoulders
		downtrend
		uptrend
After first peak	price falls below first trough before rising	inverted head and shoulders
		downtrend
	price rises from level of first trough	double bottom
		triple bottom
	price fails to reach level of first trough	uptrend
After second trough	price rises past level of first peak	double bottom
	price falls after reaching level of first peak	triple bottom
		inverted head and shoulders
	price fails to reach level of first peak	downtrend
After second peak	price falls to level of first trough and then rises	triple bottom
	price falls below level of second trough and then rises	downtrend
	price fails to reach level of second trough before rising	uptrend (distorted inverted head and shoulders)

Figure 5.2. Possible outcomes from a rising share price.

Position	Action	Possible formation
After first peak	price continues to fall	single top
	price forms a trough and then rises	double top
		triple top
		head and shoulders
		downtrend
		uptrend
After first trough	price rises above first peak before falling	head and shoulders
		uptrend
	price falls from level of first peak	double top
		triple top
	price fails to reach level of first peak	downtrend
After second peak	price falls past level of first trough	double top
	price rises after reaching level of first trough	triple top
		head and shoulders
	price fails to reach level of first trough	uptrend
After second trough	price rises to level of first peak and then falls	triple top
	price rises above level of second peak and then falls	uptrend
	price fails to reach level of second peak before falling	downtrend (distorted head and shoulders)

viewed as a distorted inverted head and shoulders with an upward sloping neckline. This will be confirmed by a rise in price through the previous resistance level. If the third trough is lower than the level of the two previous ones, then the share price is still in a downtrend, and it should be left alone.

Notice the importance of decision making at each stage of the pattern as it unfolds, the failure or success of the share price in reaching support or resistance levels leading to several possibilities for the eventual pattern which is formed. These various possibilities are summed up in Table 5.1.

The topping patterns such as single top, double top, triple top and head and shoulders can be treated in just the same way as the bottoming patterns. Once the price has fallen back from the first peak, the point at which it starts to rise again will now be a support level. It will be the fall of the price down through this support level which will indicate that the future trend is firmly downwards. If the next peak is within 5% of the position of the first peak, then the pattern could turn out to be either a double top or triple top. If the price falls from this second peak down through the resistance level then a double top has been formed, while if the price bounces back from the support level a triple top will be formed if the price reaches a peak similar to the previous two peaks before falling back down through the support level. Where the second peak is at a higher level than the outer two peaks then of course we have a head and shoulders formation. Any other possibilities will mean that the future direction of the trend is not resolved. In such cases to assume that the future direction of the share price is down may be incorrect.

The various possibilities for topping formations as the share price unfolds is shown in Table 5.2.

At this point it is necessary to draw attention once again to the distinction between bottoming patterns as a basis for buying shares and topping patterns as a basis for selling shares. Once a reversal pattern has been completed, the balance of probabilities is such that the new trend in the share price should be moving in the opposite direction. What leads to the difficulty is that the pattern is not completed until the price has pulled away from the previous resistance level in the case of bottoming patterns, and fallen below the support level in the case of topping patterns. The resistance level can be some way, perhaps 10 or 20% above the bottom price, while the support level can be a similar way below the top price. Now to give up the first 10 or 20% of a price rise is perfectly permissible when we look at the broader picture in which the rise may well take to share price to double its low value. It is not permissible to stay on board a share price which falls back by this amount from the top price. After all, there is no guarantee that the price will no suddenly plummet at any point between its top value and the support level, giving a huge, unacceptable loss.

It must be emphasised therefore that topping patterns must not be used as criteria for selling a share. Shares should be sold because they have fallen below a stop loss level, or because one of the indicators discussed later in this book is signalling that the trend has turned downwards.

CHAPTER 6

Bottoming Patterns

Because of the sustained bull market over the last ten years, even if the 1987 crash is included, there is a shortage of examples of the major bottoming formations, but plenty of the major topping formations. Even so, there are enough examples of bottoming formations to illustrate how they can be used in a practical sense.

Single bottom formations

As we pointed out in the last chapter, the simplest bottoming formation is the single bottom. This can occur as either a sharp bottom or a rounded bottom. In the case of a sharp bottom, the rapid reaction of the share price is such that an investor is rarely in a position to take advantage of it. A large proportion of the upward movement takes place over such a short time that the potential for further gain becomes limited. This is not a problem with a rounded bottom formation, which can take many months for its completion. The different problem with the rounded bottom formation, as was discussed in the last chapter, is at what level it is appropriate to make an investment. The author's view expressed earlier, is that the rounded bottom formation is best left alone as an investment opportunity unless one or other of the indicators discussed later in this book is signalling that a rise is in the offing.

A good example of a rounded bottom formation is shown in Figure 6.1 for GEC. The formation took about a year to complete, the lowest point of 144p being reached in April 1988. One way in which the rounded bottom can be highlighted as it develops is by drawing a succession of trendlines between successive important troughs. These should become less steep as the bottom of the pattern is approached, and then begin to increase in slope again.

It is extremely difficult to find a perfect example of a rounded bottom, and the one in Figure 6.1. is no exception. Thus the pattern is slightly spoiled by the fact that the price in September 1988 dipped below the trough reached at the end of July. This small fall was only temporary, and the price soon re-established its curved upward trend.

It is not necessary to use trendlines to highlight the rounded bottom formation. The outline of the rounded bottom can easily be obtained by drawing as smooth a curve as possible through the number of troughs which were formed from the beginning of 1988, as has been done in Figure 6.2. The solid line shows how this would have been done at the time that the trough in early June was formed, while the dotted line shows how the future course of the rounded bottom was estimated. The fact that the price violated this projected curve in August/September forms a useful basis for deciding on how the pattern would be treated as a buying opportunity for those investors who ignore the

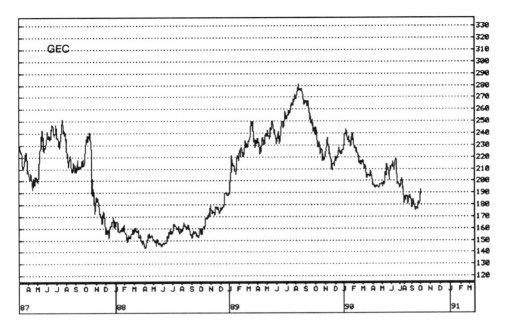

Figure 6.1. The GEC share price shows a rounded bottom formation during 1988.

advice above about using indicators to generate a buying signal. An idea of what constitutes a viable buying level can be obtained by drawing a number of levels on the chart at increasing percentage movement from the bottom level. Since this level was 144p, lines are drawn at 10% higher (158.5p), 15% higher (165.5p) and 20% higher (173p). These values are rounded to the nearest 0.5p.

As it was being formed, the trough at 155p at the end of August could have been the start of a decline, and there was no evidence either way to support the fact that the rounded bottom would continue or fail. An investor using a 10% level up from the bottom price would therefore have been at risk, since this buying level would have been triggered at the end of June, leaving him feeling quite nervous for the next three months. Another way of looking at things is that capital would have been tied up unnecessarily in a non-performing situation. Thus we can come to the conclusion, from this example, that the 10% level is not sufficiently above the base price for the curved uptrend to have become definitely established.

We now have to find another level such that there is still sufficient potential for gain, but with decreased risk. The 20% level does not satisfy this requirement, since the price level would then be 173p, which would look quite high from the historical perspective. On the other hand, the 15% level would have prevented us investing too soon, while leaving the possibility of a decent rise to come. For those investors who wish to take advantage of a rounded bottom formation, a buying level of 15% up from the lowest price reached is usually safe.

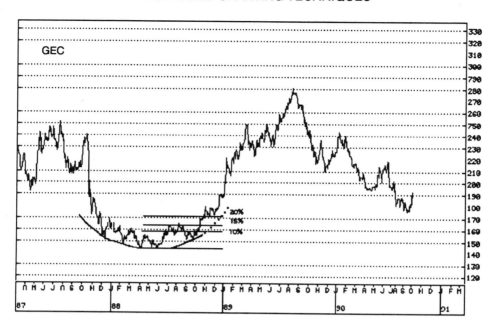

Figure 6.2. The rounded bottom is now projected into the future. The horizontal lines show levels of 10%, 15% and 20% up from the trough price.

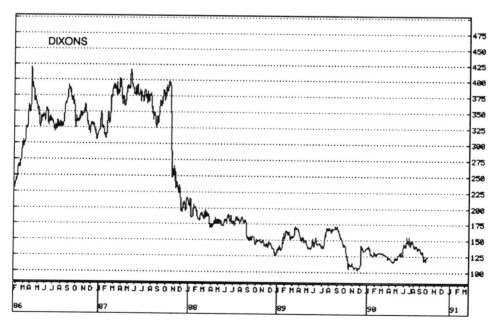

Figure 6.3. The Dixons share price is passing through a long term rounded bottom formation.

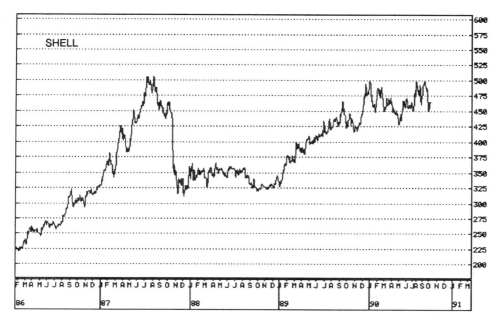

Figure 6.4. A double bottom formation in the Shell share price. The two troughs of the formation are in late 1987 and late 1988.

Sometimes a rounded bottoming formation can take many years to complete. An example is the Dixons share price following the crash of 1987. The chart in Figure 6.3 seems to bear out the fact that the lowest point was the trough in November 1989, and that the trend is now gently sloping upwards. Thus one half of the rounded bottom formation has taken two years, from November 1987 to November 1989. The practical aspect of such long drawn out patterns is that the rate of increase is too slow for them to be a good investment. For example the Dixons share price, if we are correct about the rounding bottom formation, will only have risen about 20% from its current level over the next eighteen months. This is inadequate, and much better investment opportunities can be found by the alert chartist.

Double bottom formations

These formations are rarely symmetrical, and the time gap between the two bottoms can also vary considerably. The chart of Shell in Figure 6.4 shows a double bottom pattern in which the two bottoms are about one year apart. The pattern is not symmetrical in the sense that the first bottom in October/November 1987 was formed over the course of a few weeks, being a result of the October crash. The second bottom a year later is much more rounded in form, taking several months in its formation. Interestingly, the first bottom can be seen on close examination to be a double bottom over a very short timescale, with two weeks between the two troughs. Both this set of troughs, and the second leg of the long term double bottom formation satisfy the rule that the levels to which the share price fall in each case should be within 5% of each other. The first leg fell to a lowest point of 320p and the second leg to a level of 325p.

Since there was a mini-double bottom formed during October/November 1987, the investor had to watch out for misreading the formation as being completed once the price started to rise during December 1987. In general, the closer together the two legs of the formation are, the less is the subsequent price rise out of the formation. A separation of just two weeks would certainly put this share into the category of low expectation. Thus although the price moved above the intermediate price between these two close together legs of 340p, it would not be considered for investment. The criterion to use in such cases where the two legs of a double bottom are very close together is to view it as a single bottom formation. As discussed in the section above, the critical level for buying after a single bottom is when the price has moved up by more than 15% from the bottom. In this case this would be 15% above 320p, which is 368p. The price did not rise above this point over the next few months.

After another few months the price did stagger above this 368p level, but only as far as 370p before falling back slowly. This level of 370p can be considered to be the important resistance level for any future rise. We therefore look for a significant rise above that from the second leg of the pattern. As we suggested for the rounded bottom formation, a useful level is the 15% rise from the lowest price reached during the second leg of the formation. This would put the buying level at 374p, and this level was breached by the upward moving share price during January 1989. As can be seen from the chart, the share then made a useful gain through the next six or seven months of 1989.

Note the importance of taking the long view for investment opportunities. Patience is a very important virtue for the investor who is using charting techniques. The investor would have had this share in a list of shares to watch for pattern completion from the moment the first bottom was formed, and would have kept it there for over a year before this buying opportunity arose.

Having pointed out that a gap of just two weeks is too small between the two bottoms to yield a decent investment opportunity, there is a dramatic example of a double bottom separated by about five weeks that did show a large rise. This is the behaviour of Blue Circle Industries between the time of the crash in October 1987 and the end of that year. The chart is shown in Figure 6.5. The first bottom was at 153p, while the second occurred at 148p. These are therefore within the necessary 5% of each other. The feature that makes the formation so dramatic is the excellent example of the earthquake formation, which as was pointed out previously, rises so rapidly that the investor is usually shut out until it is too late. The chart of Blue Circle is a rich source of pattern examples, since there is a head and shoulders formation present, a good example of a support line and a good example of a triangle. We shall use this chart again to illustrate these other formations.

Triple bottom formations

These are somewhat rarer than double bottom formations, probably because many triple bottoms become distorted into inverse head and shoulders patterns by the centre bottom being considerably lower than the outer two. Even when this is not the case, a

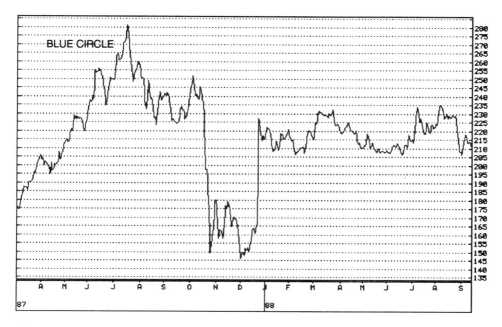

Figure 6.5. The short term double bottom formation in the Blue Circle share price.

perfectly symmetrical triple bottom is very rare. As discussed in the theoretical section, the asymmetry can be either in the distance apart of the three troughs, or in the fact that the two intermediate peaks do not rise to the same level.

The asymmetry in the height of the intermediate peaks can be seen in the example of Guardian Royal Exchange, in Figure 6.6. The first trough in late September 1986 fell to 151.5p, and the price then rose to a temporary peak of 167.5p in October. This is below our buying level of 15% up from the trough, i.e. a level of 174p, so that an investor thinking that the previous trough was a single bottom formation would not be buying the share. The price then fell back again to 151p before rising again. Once more, the investor would not buy thinking this was a double bottom formation, because this upward leg did not take the price significantly above the previously set resistance level of 167.5p. A good policy here is to wait for the price to rise by some 3% above the previous peak level before buying, and this level was of course not reached.The price fell back again to its third trough, again at 151p before rising again. On this upward leg the price did rise by more than 3% above the previous resistance of 167.5p, thereby generating a buy signal. The price then rose steadily to 190p over a few short weeks, generating a useful profit. In terms of the very close level to which each of the three bottoms descended, this share could not be beaten.

Asymmetry in the distance apart of the three bottoms, while providing a good example of symmetric intermediate peaks is provided by the chart of British Land, shown in Figure 6.7. The three troughs are within a few pence of each other, at 299p, 300p and

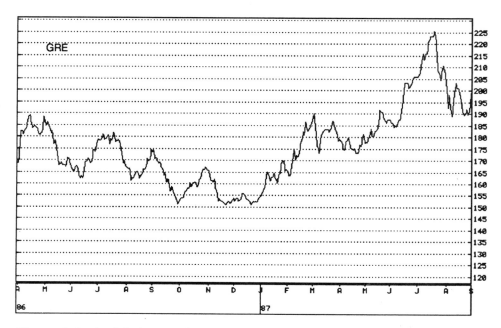

Figure 6.6. A triple bottom formation in the share price of Guardian Royal Exchange.

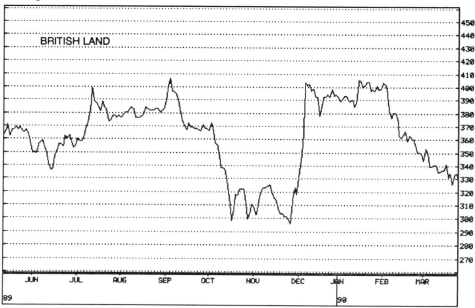

Figure 6.7. A triple bottom formation in the share price of British Land.

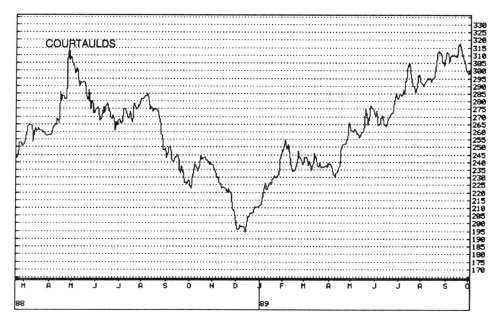

Figure 6.8. The Courtaulds share price shows an inverted head and shoulders around the low point in December 1988.

298p, thus fulfilling the basic requirement that they should be at the same level.The first intermediate peak in the middle of October 1989 rose to 322p, while the second one rose to 325p. The level of the first peak is thus less than 15% above the previous trough, so that an investor would not have taken action thinking that we had a single bottom formation. An investor would not mistake the developing formation for a double bottom, since the second peak was only a few pence higher (less than 1%) than the first peak. As pointed out above, a leeway of 2% should always be given for the rise following the second trough to guard against the possibility of a triple bottom rather than a double bottom being in progress.

Finally in early December 1989 the price rose more than 3% above the highest of the two intermediate peaks, thereby signalling the end of the triple bottom formation and indicating a buy. A very useful rise then occurred, taking the price above 400p.

The inverted head and shoulders formation

Inverted head and shoulders formations are fairly common during bear markets, but there are not so many examples over the last five years or so because of the underlying bull market for shares in general. The formation can take may weeks or even many years to complete. A typical example is shown in Figure 6.8 for Courtaulds, which lasted just over six months.

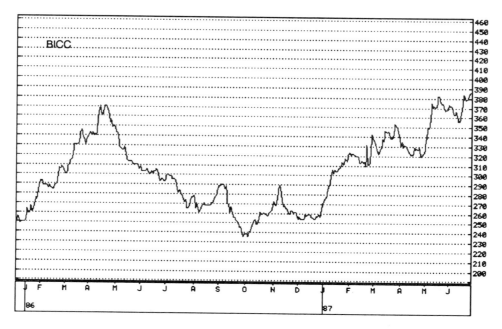

Figure 6.9. An inverted head and shoulders formation in the BICC share price.

At the beginning of the pattern, the price fell to a low point of 224p in September 1988, and bounced back from this level.The crucial level of 15% up from this at 258p was not reached, and so the investor would do nothing but continue to keep an eye on the developing pattern. The fall from this point took the price well below its previous trough of 224p to the 200p level. Not unexpectedly, since this is a 'round number' level, the price bounced back again. The investor would now begin to think in terms of a possible head and shoulders, since this second peak is well below the tolerance of within 3% of the level of the previous peak necessary for a double bottom formation. The price then rose steadily, passing the 245p level of the previous peak, reaching 255p before retracing again. The level reached by the two intermediate peaks is of course the neckline of the inverted head and shoulders, and would be horizontal for a perfectly symmetrical formation. In this present case, the neckline is therefore sloping upwards, but not at such a slope that the formation would cease to be considered an inverted head and shoulders. Note that a line joining the shoulders, i.e. joining the two troughs either side of the main trough is more or less at the same slope as the neckline. When the slopes of these two lines are markedly dissimilar, the pattern cannot really be described as a meaningful inverted head and shoulders.

The formation is not completed until the rise from the second shoulder, i.e. from a level of 240p in this case, takes the price above the neckline, i.e. above 255p. This happened in May 1989. The normal prediction for the rise in price from this point at which the neckline is broken is for an amount similar to the price difference between the lowest point of the central peak, i.e. 200p, to the right-hand neckline, i.e. 255p. This should therefore take the price to about 310p. This forecast was uncannily correct, since the price reached 312p before falling back again.

Another example of a short term inverted head and shoulders formation can be seen in the BICC chart in Figure 6.9. This occurred between June and December 1986. The inverted head falls significantly below the level of the inverted shoulders, and the extremely well defined neckline is almost exactly horizontal, i.e. the two intermediate peaks are at the same level. Exit from the pattern led to a very useful rise in the share price over the next year, terminated by a double top formation in the autumn of 1987.

Buying Rules

1. First trough.

If price rises by 15% from the lowest point then formation is probably a rounded bottom and investor can buy.

2. Second trough.

If price at second trough is within 3% of that of the first trough then formation is either double bottom or triple bottom. If price then rises above level of the peak price between the first and second troughs the formation is a double bottom and investor can buy, otherwise wait for triple bottom pattern development.

3. Second trough.

If price at second trough is lower than that of the first trough then formation is probably an inverted head and shoulders. Investor should wait for pattern development.

4. Third trough.

If price level is within 3% of that of the first trough then triple bottom or head and shoulders probable. If triple bottom then investor should wait for price to rise above level of highest of the two intermediate peaks before buying. If inverted head and shoulders then wait for price to rise above neckline (the line joining the tops of the two intermediate peaks) before buying.

5. Third trough.

If price level is not within 3% of that of the first trough then move to another share.

CHAPTER 7

Topping Patterns

Unlike the situation with bottoming patterns, charts of the last ten years of share price histories are rich with examples of topping patterns. There are many instances of single tops, rounded tops, double tops, triple tops and head and shoulders. Even so, a perfect symmetrical example of any of these patterns is still rare, and there are usually slight differences from perfection. The approach to these topping patterns is virtually a mirror image of that employed for the bottoming formations, with similar rules being employed about the extent to which a price should fall back from the top, and how close together multiple tops have to be, etc.

Single top formations

All rounded top formations, and indeed all rounded bottom formations, will be slightly distorted by the presence of fluctuations of much shorter duration than the formation itself. A good example is that of Smithkline Beecham, shown in Figure 7.1. A line drawn so as to touch the minor peaks that occur between the end of January 1989 and October 1989 is obviously a rounded curve. Instead of a such a curve, it is also possible to draw fan lines, which exhibit a gradual reduction in their slopes until the slopes change direction as the top of the formation is passed. The lines then get increasingly steep again. The clean pattern is rather spoilt by the steep fall that occurred in July, but the price bounced back within a month to a level that maintained the overall rounded curve. Since the peak price reached was 650p, the significant 15% fall is at a price of 552.5p. Therefore, with a rounded top formation, the probability is for a further fall once the price falls to this level. If it does not fall this far, then the pattern may turn out to be a double top, triple top or head and shoulders. As far as the extent of a fall from a rounded top formation is concerned, for a symmetrical top the expectation has to be for a fall to the general level of the share price before the rise to the top occurred.

In the present example, the price fell past the 552.5p level and reached 518p before rising again. Thus the price fall is not quite as much as might have been expected, since the level of the price before the rounded top, during the last quarter of 1988 was about 470p.

As shown in Figure 7.2, it is possible to take a more flexible view of the pattern, where the trough in November 1989 is considered to be an aberration of a rounded top formation which was not completed until the middle of 1990. In this case the price has come down to the 480-490p mark, so that this top can be considered to be much more symmetrical as far as the beginning and ending price levels are concerned.

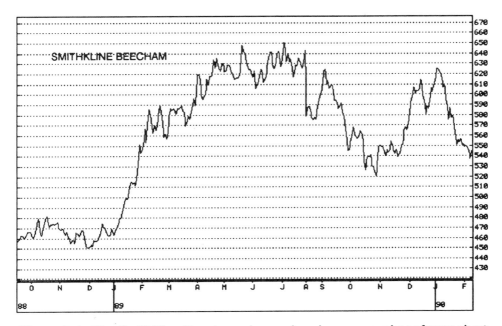

Figure 7.1. The Smithkline Beecham share price shows a number of very short term cycles superimposed on a rounded top formation.

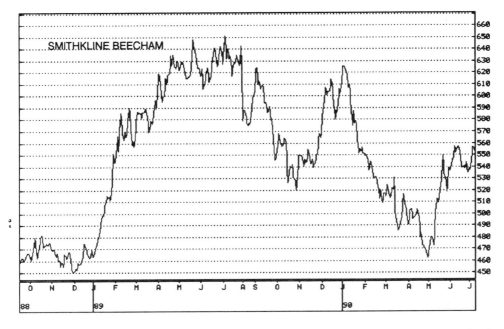

Figure 7.2. The rounded top formation can now be seen to include the peak of December 1990. The start of the formation is in December 1988 and the end in April 1990.

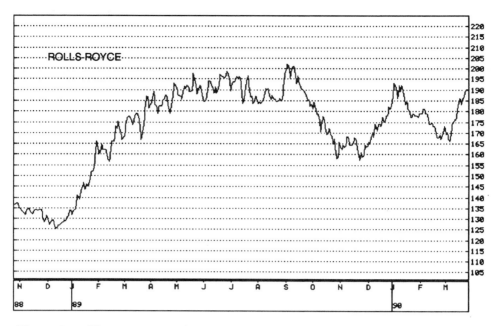

Figure 7.3. The symmetry of a rounded top formation in the Rolls-Royce share price is disturbed by the price rise in August 1989.

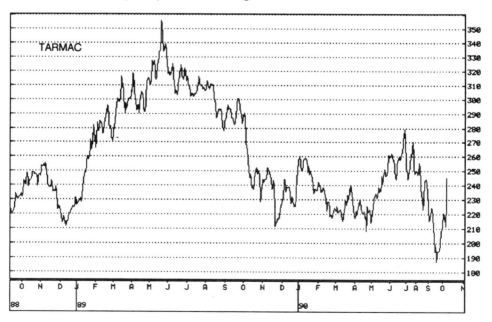

Figure 7.4. The rounded top formation in the Tarmac share price has a sharp top formation superimposed on it.

A good example of a rounded top which is extremely well defined until just after the peak price is that shown in Figure 7.3 for Rolls Royce. All the requirements are there: a good rise from a low point of about 130p in December 1988, a gradually curving formation broken only by the well-contained short term fluctuations, and a recognisable top at 200p. By mid-August 1989 the price was down to 185p, still not 15% down from the top, but looking more and more like a good symmetrical formation. The whole pattern was then somewhat spoilt by a rise back up to 200p before the price collapsed over the next two months to 161p, still well above the price level of 130p which from which the rise to the top started.

These two examples show the difficulty with rounded top formations - perfectly symmetrical ones are quite rare, and ones which look good bets for behaving perfectly usually show an erratic behaviour just after the top has passed, and usually before the fall of 15% is reached. For this reason, and this has been stated many times, investors are not encouraged to take major investment decisions based simply on a developing rounded top pattern. This comment is really aimed at traded options investors, since an investor in shares must use a stop loss method to generate a selling signal, and not wait for any of the topping formations to be completed.

Tarmac (Figure 7.4) provides an interesting example of a combination of a rounded top and sharp top during the period January to July 1989. If the spike top is ignored, a nicely rounded pattern can be drawn with its maximum at about 330p in May. Where this maximum would have occurred was an excellent example of a spike, since the price rose rapidly by 10% to 360p in the course of a few days. The rapidity of the consequent fall was such that no technical analysis system could get the investor out anywhere near the top, although the price then stayed for a short while at the level which it would be passing through in its way through the underlying rounded top.

Double top formations

There are many examples of double tops over the last few years. The patterns can be long term, in the sense that the tops are more than a year apart, or they can be relatively short term, the tops being but a few weeks apart. The main criterion is that the price levels of the two tops should be within 3% of each other.

The Reed International share price as shown in Figure 7.5 is an excellent and intriguing example of an intermediate term double top, since the two tops are only just over three months apart. The classic condition of a good run up in the share price is present, since the price moved from around 150p at the beginning of 1986 to a peak level of 612p in June 1987. The price fell back to 500p in August before making another attempt at the peak. This reached 621p in September 1987 before falling back slightly over the next few days. The formation is intriguing because although the crash occurred just a week or so later, it is arguable that the double top formation was already in being at the time of the crash, and was not a result of the crash. Note again the classic situation as regards the fall back from the second peak. The normal expectation is for a fall below the level of the intermediate trough of at least as great as the level which the trough is below the peak. Since the trough is at 500p, and therefore 121p down from the peak, we would expect the fall to be 121p down from the trough, i.e. at 500p - 121p = 389p.

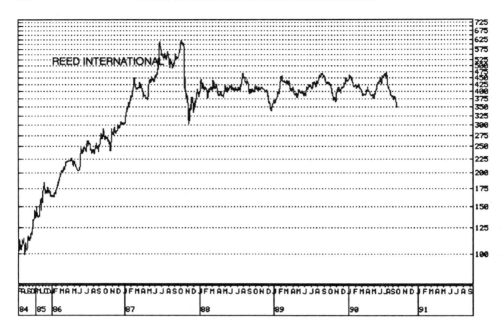

Figure 7.5. The share price of Reed International shows a double top formation in 1987.

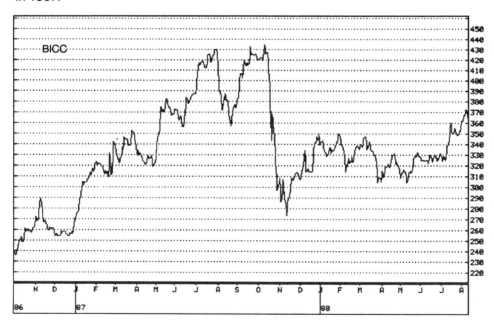

Figure 7.6. The BICC share price also has a double top in 1987.

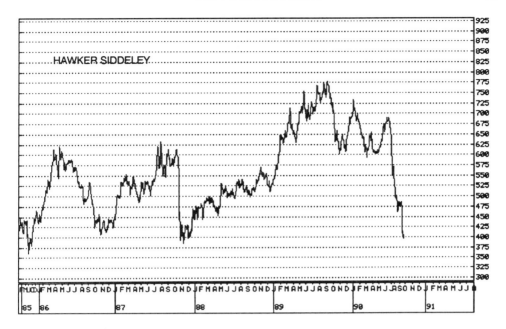

Figure 7.7. Following the double top formation in Hawker Siddeley in 1986 and 1987, the price did not fall below the intermediate trough.

Although difficult to see on the larger scale exactly what happened, it is clear that there was a hesitation at this level before the share price fell again to just above 300p.

A look at any chart book which covers the period since the beginning of 1986 shows that quite a high proportion of the shares showed distorted double tops at the time of the crash, and a considerable number showed good double tops that were not distorted. As in the case of Reed International, these double tops had already been formed just prior to the crash, and this raises all kinds of philosophical questions which this author is unable to answer. It seems difficult to grasp the fact that the crash occurred exactly at a time when a large number of shares were standing almost exactly level with a peak reached only a few months earlier. As another example, the chart of BICC is shown again in Figure 7.6. The first peak took the price to 425p in June 1987, and the price then retreated to 370p before climbing again to 426p in September. The minimum fall to be expected from this second peak would be 52p down from the central trough, i.e. at 318p, by analogy with the Reed case and the general expectation for the fall from a double top. Again on the chart can be seen a little hesitation at that level in mid-October before further panic on the part of investors took the price down further to 276p in late October.

Quite a proportion of double top formations fail to make the expected fall, and sometimes even show a rise. An example here is Hawker Siddeley, shown in Figure 7.7. Although the double top is not as clean as it could be, it is still obvious as such, with a peak price being reached of 625p in April 1986 and 630p in August 1987. This is therefore a long term double top formation. The interesting aspect is that during the October crash

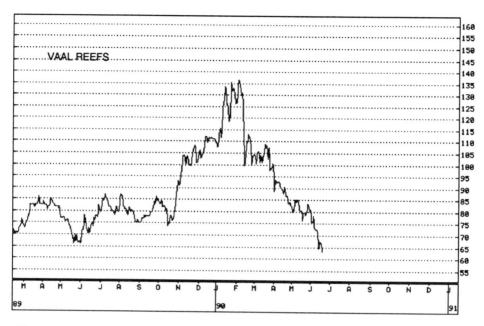

Figure 7.8. A good example of a short term triple top in Vaal Reefs.

the price only just fell below the intermediate trough of 425p, rather than down to the expected level of 225p. The price then rose fairly steadily over the next two years to 770p before falling back again. On closer inspection the reason for the failure can be seen. The starting point for the rise through the double top formation was around 425p, and the intermediate trough fell all the way back to this starting level. Thus this starting level acts as a loosely defined support area, so that when the crash took the price back down towards it, the price failed to penetrate, and bounced back up again.

Besides this type of failure where there is an obvious explanation, there are still plenty of failures where everything would seem to be correct for a normal double top pattern - there is a good rise to the first peak, the intermediate trough is still some way above the original starting level, and the second peak is within 3% of the level of the first peak. It can still happen that the fall from the second peak takes the price only marginally below the level of the intermediate trough before rising again. Even so, on the balance of probabilities, a well defined double top formation should lead to a significant fall in the share price.

Triple top

A perfectly symmetrical triple top formation is extremely rare. Most triple tops become distorted into a head and shoulders pattern, but examples of triple tops with lesser distortion do exist.

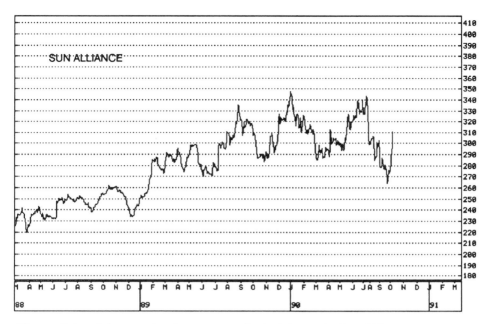

Figure 7.9. An example of an asymetrical triple top in Sun Alliance.

The four requirements for a perfect triple top are:

- The price should have risen substantially
- The levels of the tops should be within 3% of each other
- The intermediate troughs should be at similar levels
- The three peaks should be equally spaced in time

The first two of these are essential if the pattern is to be considered to be a triple top. Most triple top formations will fail to satisfy either the third or fourth requirements, and some will fail on both of these.

A good example of a triple top that satisfies requirements 1, 2 and 4 is to be found with Vaal Reefs, as shown in Figure 7.8. The pattern is a short term one, the three peaks occurring over the course of one month. They are equally spaced in time, and the only distortion is that the troughs are not at similar levels. In fact, because the troughs are on a rising line and the peaks are also on a rising line of lesser slope, the pattern can be considered to be a wedge, which will be discussed in a later chapter.

The triple top succeeds admirably in that the fall from the final peak is twice the distance from the peak to the lowest of the two troughs. Underlying the triple top formation is a rounded top, and this carries the price down further from the effect of the

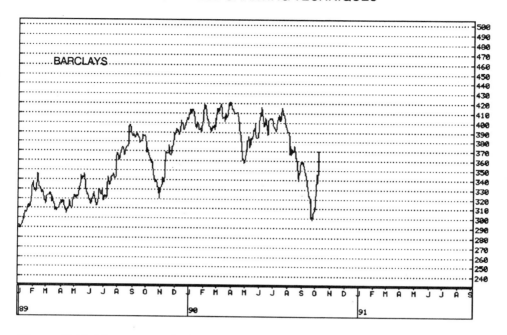

Figure 7.10. There are multiple tops in the Barclays share price.

triple top. The net result is that the price halved in a period of just six months, giving fabulous profits to the traded options investor.

In the case of Sun Alliance (Figure 7.9), the peaks from autumn 1989 to summer 1990 are within 3% of each other and the troughs are within a penny of each other at 284p and 285p. The peaks are not quite equally spaced in time. The price has also run up very nicely from just below 200p following the crash of 1987, although the run up is rather sinuous. At the time of writing the triple top formation seems to have been completed, with the final fall below the intermediate trough being much less than expected.

Multiple tops

Occasionally patterns can be seen which have more than three peaks at about the same price level. These are best referred to as multiple tops. Symmetrical examples where all troughs are at the same general level and the peaks are equally spaced in time are virtually never seen, but the short term multiple top shown by Barclays in late 1989/early 1990 is probably as close to the ideal that will be seen. The multiple top followed the necessary long run up in price from just below 450p in October to 580p in January, and the peaks are almost perfectly spaced in time as well as being within less than 3% of each other as regards price.

Since the lowest troughs were at 550p, the projection would be for a fall from the final peak at 590p of 80p, i.e. down to 510p. The price did fall rapidly in April to a level of 505p before recovering a little more than half of this loss.

Selling rules

In the last chapter a number of buying rules were listed for the various bottoming formations. The logic here was that once the bottoming formation was complete, the investor should be able to forward to a rise in price, and therefore the situation was one of low risk and high potential for profit. The situation with topping formations is quite different, since by the time they have been completed and the price is in a downtrend the fall from the top is already considerable. As an example, taking the Barclays case above, the price will have fallen from 590p down to 550p just to take the price down to the level of the intermediate troughs. This is a fall of 6.8%, and a much lesser loss in price from the peak price can be obtained by the use of stop losses. For this reason, no selling rules will be presented here.

CHAPTER 8

Trending Patterns

The previous two chapters concerned reversal patterns, where as the pattern unfolds, an upper or lower limit to the price trend becomes obvious. The expectation is then for the price trend to reverse direction. This chapter discusses trending patterns, where as long as the pattern unfolds, the trend is continuing, and the point at which the trend will reverse is unknown. Technical analysis is bedevilled by the misuse of mathematics and indeed the misuse of English. Thus is would be logical to call the trending patterns which will be discussed in this chapter 'continuation patterns', since it is readily established that the trend being examined is continuing. Unfortunately in technical analysis this term has a rather different meaning, and applies to situations where the trend of the price after the pattern is in the same direction as the trend of the price before the pattern rather than applying to the behaviour of the price within the pattern. A much better term for these situations would be 'hesitation patterns', because there is a period of hesitation and uncertainty before the trend is re-established, and the term is self-explanatory.

It seems rather meaningless to state that a trending pattern will continue until it ends, but the point is that we can focus on the pattern in such a way that as soon as it does end, we know that it has ended. We are thus able to take the appropriate investment action at an early stage. The trends discussed in this chapter are of two types, simple uptrends and downtrends and trends which are contained within a channel. Either of these types can be straight or curved.

Simple trends

Straight Uptrend

Legal and General provide an excellent example (Figure 8.1) of a straight uptrend which persisted for over two years. The uptrend started as a reaction to the rapid price fall at the time of the crash in October 1987, and incredibly is still in being at the time of writing. As shown in Figure 8.1, a straight trendline can be drawn so as to touch exactly the troughs at December 1987, December 1988 and April 1990. In a perfect world, the troughs at May 1988 and May/June 1989 would also touch the line, but a small amount of tolerance either side of the trendline is acceptable. Thus the troughs can fall slightly short of the trendline, as in this case, or penetrate it slightly.

With such a pattern it is obvious that while any new troughs that are formed fall within the allowed tolerance either side of the trendline, the uptrend is still in being, and the investor can ride with it. The key to good profits is of course the ability to recognise such uptrends early in their development so as to benefit for as long as possible from the rise.

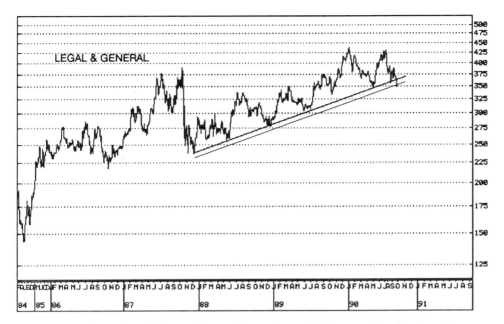

Figure 8.1. Legal and General provide and excellent example of a long term up-trend. A line is drawn at a constant 5% below the trendline. Once the price breaks down through this, the trend is considered to be broken.

The key to retaining such good profits is to be able to recognise when such a trend has ended so as to exit with a large proportion of the accumulated profit. The time of highest risk is when the share price is rapidly approaching the extrapolated trendline after falling back from one of the intermediate peaks. Since we have said that a slight tolerance is allowable, it is not correct to sell when the price touches the trendline, since during the time the uptrend has been in being, the share price has consistently bounced back up from it. The amount of penetration of the price down through the trendline which is allowable before the trend is considered to have been broken is then crucial. Most technical analysts settle for a 5% penetration of the trendline.

At the last point on the chart in Figure 8.1, the price was at 365p, almost exactly on the projected trendline. It is necessary therefore for the price to fall to 346p before it can be said that the uptrend is broken and it is time to sell.

An advantage of a logarithmic scale over a linear scale for displaying trendlines is that it is slightly easier to draw a second line at a distance of 5% below it since this distance will be a constant. The 5% line will therefore be parallel to the original trendline. In the case of linear charts the gap between the trendline and the line 5% below it will get large as the price moves higher, although the line will still be straight. Such a 5% line is shown on the logarithmic chart of Figure 8.1. It is a penetration of the share price through this line, even by an amount as small as 0.5p that is the signal that the uptrend has ended.

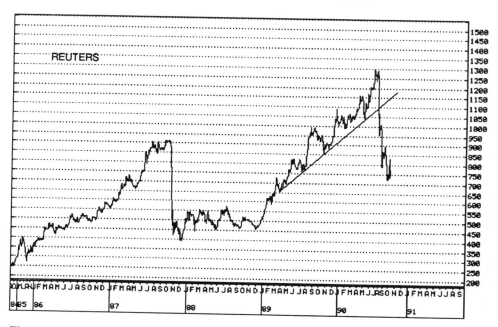

Figure 8.2. The penetration of the downtrend in the Reuters share price led to a substantial fall.

Note the major difference between a simple uptrend and a channelled uptrend: although the troughs all lie on a straight trendline, no such line can be drawn through the intermediate peaks. The peaks are at irregular heights above the rising trendline.

The chart of Reuters shown in Figure 8.2 is a dramatic example of penetration of an uptrend line. The uptrend started at the beginning of 1989, and four troughs lie almost exactly on it. The price suffered an almost vertical fall from its peak of 1290p on July 12th, which took it down to 1060p by the 30th, well below the level of the trendline at this point, which was at 1120p. In view of the length of the uptrend being well over one year in duration at this point, the share was in a high risk situation. This is one of the occasions where an absolute rule seems to be so accurate as to leave the investor wondering whether it is all pre-ordained, since the point 5% down from the trendline price of 1120p is 1064p, and the share price had penetrated this only marginally. The psychology of many investors at this point is such that they would dither, being absolutely convinced that such a steep fall had to be followed by a rapid bounce back. The few days that the price spent in this region would only confirm to them that it would be better to hang on than sell, since the share price seemed to be gathering steam for a retracement or at least partial retracement of the fall. However, the rules that are given here stand the test of time, since they are usually, but not always, correct. There is no technical analysis reason why the share should not have been sold at this point. In fact, when the section on flags in the next chapter is reached, the few days spent at the 1060p level would indicate that the share was passing through only a brief moment of hesitation before falling further.

Figure 8.3. The uptrend in the Rolls-Royce share price has been maintained for three years.

The correctness of this selling strategy can be seen from the last few days of the chart, since the share price fell even more drastically, by nearly 30% in a very short time.

Again, the key to profit in this Reuters example is to get into the uptrend early. An investor should have been able to recognise that an uptrend was in being during July 1989, when the price moved upwards from the trough at just below 800p. This trough was almost in a straight line with the two previous troughs in February and March 1989. Thus a useful gain could have been obtained from this level of 800p.

Comparison of the two charts, Legal and General with Reuters can be used to emphasise a point about the length of trends. In general, the gentler the upward slope of the trendline, the longer does it continues upwards. Thus in the Legal and General case, the trend has lasted nearly three years, and is still in being. The trendline has moved from about 240p to 360p in that time, a rise of 50% in three years. The Reuters trendline moved from about 640p to 1130p, a rise of 76% in about eighteen months.

Probably the limit in the rate of climb of a trendline versus the length of time for which it continues is reached by Rolls Royce, as shown in Figure 8.3. The uptrend started with the fall in October 1987, and five points lie on it, the latest being in March 1990. The trendline itself has moved from 100p in October 1987 to 167p at the last trough in 1990, a climb of 76% in two and a quarter years. Note the excellent example, mentioned earlier, of a rounded top pattern being formed in 1989.

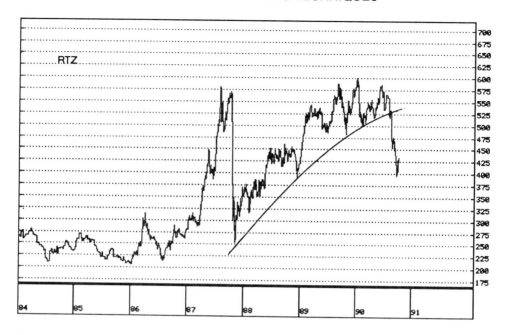

Figure 8.4. A curved uptrend can be drawn on the RTZ chart. The curvature is gradually decreasing, and the trend was broken in August 1990.

Curved Uptrend

A curved uptrend differs from a straight uptrend by virtue of the fact that the troughs all lie on curve. Although a curve can be drawn through any three troughs, a curved uptrend is much better defined if at least four troughs lie on it. The rule for deciding that the trend has come to an end is not quite the same as that for straight uptrends, since the curvature of the trendline plays an additional part.

A good example can be found in the price for RTZ over the last three years, as shown in Figure 8.4. The major troughs at October 1987, December 1988 and September 1989 all lie on a curved line whose curvature is decreasing. The next trough in January 1990 lies on the best projection of the curve onwards from the trough in September 1989, and at this point the price would be watched very carefully for signs of falling significantly below the trendline. A major advantage of curved trendlines over straight ones is that there is another signal that the end of the trend is coming closer, and that is when the curve is flattening out. Thus in the present case, the next trough in April 1990 forced the curve to continue to flatten out, thus making the investor more aware that the next time the price fell back to the trendline could be the end of the trend. In July the price did fall back to a position slightly below the projected trendline at 525p and spent a few days hesitating at this level. Unlike the straight trendline, where the investor would still hang on because the price was not 5% below the trendline, a critical fact is that the price had fallen just a penny or so below that of the previous trough. This indicated that the curved

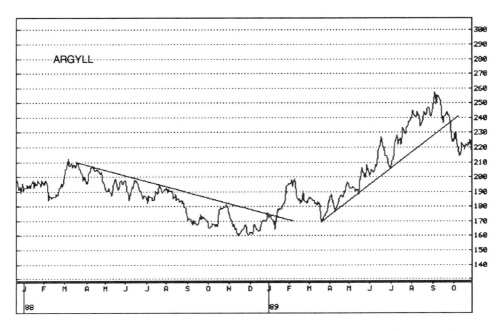

Figure 8.5. The Argyll Group share price is a good example of a downtrend turning into an uptrend.

trendline had passed its peak, and it was therefore time to sell. Note another indication of a continued fall in the small flag which this period of hesitation had formed (see next chapter). For those who missed the first signal this flag gave a last chance to sell. The price then collapsed rapidly to a level of just over 400p, justifying the selling decision.

Straight Downtrend

As mentioned earlier in this book, downtrend lines are constructed by drawing a straight line through three or more peaks. The chart of Argyll Group shown in Figure 8.5 is a good example of a downtrend changing into an uptrend. The downtrend lasted for most of 1988, and the trendline can be seen to have begun with the peak of 210p on 18th March 1988. By April it was possible to construct the trendline through three successive peaks. Although the next bunch of peaks in May and June were somewhat below the level of the projected line, the next peak in July at 194p was exactly on this line. The price fell away again and it was another three months before the same trendline was picked up again. The next peak on 29th December at 175p was the sixth point lying on the line, giving an unusually well defined trend. In such a situation a breaking of the trend by 5% is very significant. The price fell away slightly from this peak to a low point of 164p on the 16th January 1989 and then rose sharply to a level of 182p to penetrate the line. This represents exactly 5% above the trendline itself, and in view of the strength of the line with six peaks on it can be considered to be an unambiguous signal that the

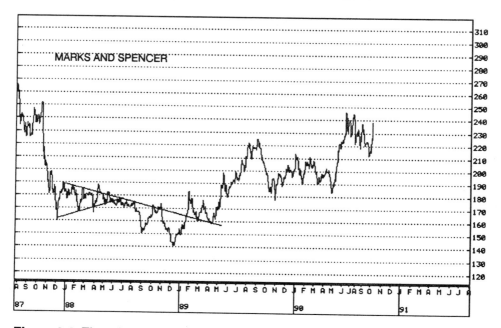

Figure 8.6. There is a well defined downtrend in the Marks and Spencer share price with a large number of peaks lying on the line.

downtrend has been broken. The correctness of this view is supported by the fact that the price rose rapidly to 198p on the 8th February. The low point of 16th January was a major low, being the lowest point reached in the last five years.

By March 1989 the price retreated to the first of an series of troughs which formed a new major uptrend which took the price up to an all time high in August 1989.

Note the all important difference between a downtrend and downchannel. It is not possible to draw a straight line through the troughs, since they are at irregular price levels. For a down channel, as will be seen shortly, it is possible to draw another line through the troughs which is parallel to the line through the peaks.

A good example of a short term downtrend with a difference can be found in the Marks and Spencer share price, as shown in Figure 8.6. The fairly gentle downtrend lasted for about a year from December 1987, following the more drastic fall during the October crash. It can be seen that quite a few very short term peaks lie on the line. It can also be seen that one or two peaks stand a little bit proud of the line. The reason is that with so many peaks - about ten in all - occurring over such a relatively short time period, it is unrealistic to expect total perfection with all of them lying exactly in a straight line. The important point is that the peaks that do violate the line do not do so by 5%, and therefore they do not signal that the trend is broken. It is perfectly in order to continue the trendline through these peaks, picking up further peaks which do lie on the line.

The reason for stating that this downtrend is different is that for much of the duration of the trend the troughs can be loosely connected by a straight line, but since this is not parallel to the downtrend, we do not have a down channel. The two lines are at a converging angle and the resulting partial pattern is a triangle of a type which will be discussed in the next chapter.

Once the triangular part of the pattern is in the past, it can be seen that the peaks in October and November 1988 still fall on this trendline. The trendline is not penetrated by the necessary 5% on the upside until January 1989. At that point a very interesting thing happens. The downtrend line, which can also be considered to be a resistance line in the sense that while it is in being the price is unable to move above it, then becomes a support line, in the sense that the price is unable to fall below it. Thus in February and April the price falls towards the projected trendline and then bounces back up without penetrating down through it. In a later chapter we discuss the concept of support and resistance lines, a feature of which can be that a resistance line often turns into a support line. The difference in this example is that while support and resistance lines are horizontal, this is a rare example of such a line which is sloping.

Curved Downtrend

In the Beazer share price shown in Figure 8.7 a curved downtrend can be seen which was maintained for the period April to November 1989. The curve is well defined by having six peaks lying on it, from the initial peak in April to the final peak in early November. The last peak, at 162p is also part of an inverted head and shoulders formation with its inverted head reaching down to 125p in October. The rebound from the curved trendline in November was of short lived duration, since the price then rose up through the curve within a few days.

Unlike the curved uptrend discussed earlier, where the curve was flattening out, and the investor could be more relaxed about the 5% rule, in the Beazer case the curved downtrend line is increasing in curvature. Thus the curve itself is not giving any indication that the trend is ending other than the fact that once the curve is nearly vertical the price is in free fall and must therefore come to an end within a few days. In the present case the slope is not that steep, so the investor has only the 5% rule to aid him and must apply it rigorously. When the price rose through the trendline, it took only a few days to reach a level of 149p, which is more than 5% above the trendline. This is therefore a signal to buy. Looking at the short term, the price rose from this level of 149p to 177p by the beginning of January for an 18% rise in just over 6 weeks, justifying the view that the downtrend had come to an end once the curve was violated.

Channelled trends

Channelled trends are uptrends and downtrends in which the excursions away from the trendline are limited by another line which is at a constant distance from the trendline. In the uptrends and downtrends discussed earlier, the excursions were not limited, so that the trends appeared to be somewhat irregular. As with simple trends, channelled trends can be straight or curved.

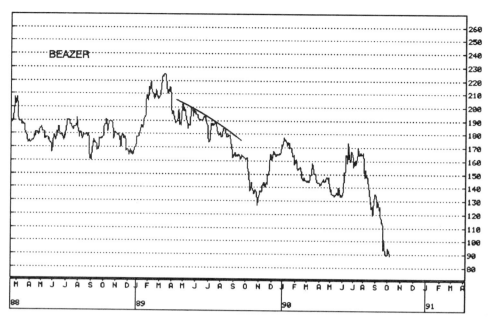

Figure 8.7. A curved downtrend can be seen for the first half of 1989 in the Beazer chart.

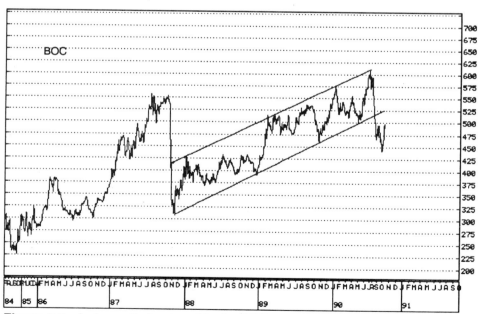

Figure 8.8. A channelled uptrend in the BOC share price.

Straight upchannel

The share price of BOC in Figure 8.8 shows the existence of a channelled uptrend of over two years of persistence. The lower boundary has four troughs which lie almost exactly on it, the first such trough being the one due to the October 1987 crash and the final trough being in March 1990. That we have a channel rather than a simple uptrend is readily observed , since the upper boundary can be drawn so that the four greatest excursions from the trendline lie on it. The first such peak was in December 1987, while the latest one was in May 1990. The price fell back somewhat from this upper boundary during July 1990 and then reached the lower boundary which was at a level of 520p in early August. The price continued down past the 5% below the boundary level within a few days, giving a clear signal that the end of the uptrend had come. That this was correct was shown by the fall of the price to 462p by mid-August.

It is important that as was the case with simple uptrends, investors do not use the fall of 5% below the lower boundary as a selling signal. Many channels are of large depth, so that the fall when a share price peaks at the upper boundary and drops to the lower boundary can be large. For example in the present case the price peaked at 610p and then fell within a very short period of time to the lower boundary at 520p, i.e. a fall of nearly 15%. Taking an extra 5% below the lower boundary takes the fall to 19% from the peak price. The only way in which penetration of the lower boundary of a channelled uptrend should be used is as an indication that the price is now headed on a downtrend, of indeterminate length. As will be seen in the chapter on Channel Analysis, a close study of the behaviour of price movement within channels can be extremely rewarding in terms of much sharper timing of buying and selling points.

Curved Upchannel

Curved channelled trends are equally as common as straight ones, and the chart of Ladbroke in Figure 8.9 shows such a curved uptrend running over most of 1988. A lower boundary can be drawn through five troughs, starting with the trough immediately after the fall in October 1987 and ending with the trough in December 1988. A curved upper boundary can also be drawn to cover the same time period and passing through the peaks in March 1988, July 1988 and September 1988. By the end of 1988 the curve was quite obviously flattening out, and therefore the investor would be expecting the end of the uptrend to be signalled by a breakout through the upper boundary. Perversely the breakout was through the upper boundary in January 1989. What this means is that the short term uptrend was replaced by a much stronger longer term uptrend, which took the share price up much more rapidly. The price eventually peaked out at around 350p before a series of short term cycles came into prominence which were superimposed on the stronger uptrend which was now topping out.

Straight downchannel

A recent version of a downchannel which was dramatically penetrated on the downside is provided by the share price of Burton Group (Figure 8.10). The first trough which can be said to lie on the downward-sloping lower boundary is at the beginning of

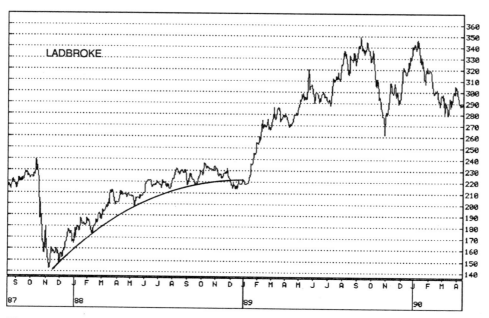

Figure 8.9. A curved uptrend can be seen over most of 1988 in the Ladbroke share price.

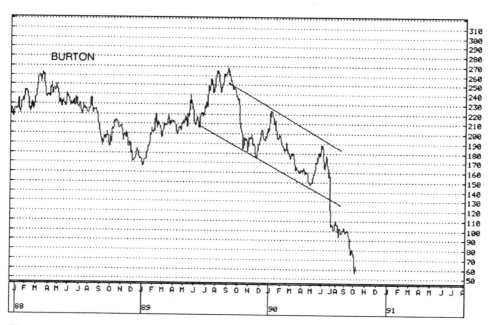

Figure 8.10 . A straight downchannel in the Burton share price.

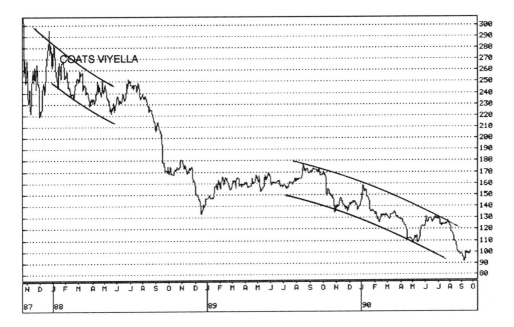

Figure 8.11. There are two curved downchannels in Coats Viyella.

June 1989, and the second one occurred in November of that year. Once this line was drawn in, the peaks in September and December 1989 could be seen to lie on a line which was reasonably parallel to the original downtrend line, the two lines now forming a downchannel. The share price fell back from this December peak to arrive at the lower boundary in April 1990, again bouncing back up rapidly towards the upper boundary again. This was reached in June 1990, and the price rebounded downwards extremely rapidly on a course which took it through the lower boundary which was then at 135p, and right down to the 100p level without so much as a breathing space. This is a case similar to that of Ladbroke, but in an opposite sense. The moderately steep downtrend is replaced rapidly by a much steeper downtrend.

Curved downchannel

Coats Viyella, shown on Figure 8.11 is interesting because of the existence of two curved downchannels, a short term one and a medium term one. The first of these, the short term channel can be seen from late 1987 to mid 1988. It is very well defined, having four troughs lying on the lower boundary, and five peaks lying on the upper boundary. This is one of those cases where it is essential to wait for a break through a boundary before taking any investment decision. Quite obviously, the channel is a curve that is flattening out, and so there is every indication that the price should start to rise again. Those investors who by their nature have a tendency to jump the gun would come to grief, because they would be totally convinced that once the price had reached the bottom of the channel in August 1988 the only way it could go would be upwards. As will be seen from the chapter on Channel Analysis, such premature action is never to be taken, and confirmation that a channel has passed its bottom point must be seen before action is taken. In the case of Coats Viyella, the investor would see that there is no bounce back from the bottom of the channel, and the price fell down through it. The conclusion therefore is that the gradually straightening downtrend has been replaced by a much more severe downtrend, and no investment would have been made at that point.

Once the share price had climbed back slightly from the trough in December 1988, the share entered a new channelled trend which again was curving downwards, but with a curve that had passed its maximum rather than, as was the case with the short term channel a curve that was approaching its minimum. Thus at the time of writing, the indication is that the share price at 97p is now at the lower boundary of this downchannel. Thus it has to be watched to see if it bounces back or penetrates the lower boundary to enter an even steeper downtrend.

CHAPTER 9

Hesitation Patterns

The patterns which will be discussed here are often gathered together under the term "continuation patterns", but this is a misnomer, since many of the patterns are in an ambiguous state where they can continue the previous trend or reverse it. A much better term is that used for the title of this chapter, "hesitation patterns", since the term is then self-explanatory. The share price is in a phase in which it is making up its mind about its future direction, and the future direction is not known until a breakout from the pattern occurs. Except for the special case of flags, these patterns can be of medium or short term. Flag patterns are periods of hesitation which last for up to a few weeks, usually taken to be about three weeks maximum, and are therefore special cases of these more general hesitation patterns.

Support/Resistance lines

Support lines are horizontal lines from which the share price repeatedly bounces back upwards. Resistance lines are lines from which the share price repeatedly bounces back downwards. The reason for bracketing these two together in this heading is that it very often happens that once a resistance line is violated, it then becomes a support line, and once a support line is violated it then becomes a resistance line.

While two or three troughs can fall to exactly the same value and two or three peaks rise to the same value, giving an exactly horizontal support or resistance line, it is unusual for many more troughs or peaks to fall exactly on the line. For these extended cases a small amount of tolerance is to be expected, but this should be no more than two or three percent of the level of the line in question. This is exemplified by the share price of Land Securities (Figure 9.1) through most of 1988 and 1989. There is obviously a line of resistance at about 600p above which the share price has failed to hold despite numerous attempts during this period of time. The first peak at the start of this resistance was on the 20th May 1988 at 596p. The price fell back slightly before having another go at this level a few weeks later, this time advancing slightly to 598p on the 15th June. It was another five months before a third attempt was made on this level, and this time the price broke through to 609p on the 23rd November. Since this is only 2% above the first of these attempts, it cannot be considered that the line has been broken, and this was confirmed by the fact that the price then fell back once again. A new attempt was made in February 1989 which took the price up to a peak of 600p, but again this failed to make a decisive breakthrough. Several further efforts in March and May took the price to 593p and 596p before the price rose to 609p on the 12th April 1989. By this time the view would have been formed that the real resistance line was at 600p, and that the very small

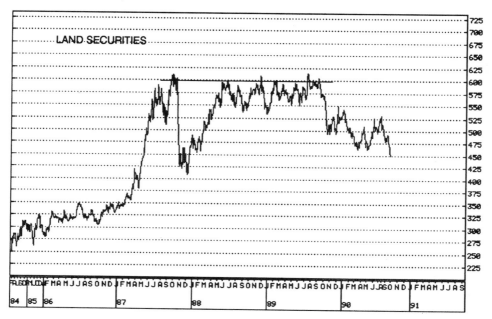

Figure 9.1. A resistance line at 600p in Land Securities.

penetrations were simply a random fluctuation about this line. Thus a rise to 609p represents a rise of only 1.5% through this line, and cannot be considered to be significant. Sure enough, the price fell back again before reaching the 600p level again on the 17th August. Finally the price struggled to 605p on the 5th September 1989 before giving up and falling away rapidly to below 500p.

Thus the history of the Land Securities share price is one of numerous attempts to cross the 600p level decisively and of constant failure to do this. Since a resistance line may be considered to be a horizontal trendline, we have to adopt the same criterion for penetration as we did with trendlines: the price has to penetrate the resistance line by 5% before we can consider that the resistance has been broken.

An example where there have been fewer attempts to cross a resistance line, but where the line has still stayed valid for almost two years can be seen in Reed International (Figure 9.2). Nearly one year after the October 1987 crash the price had recovered about half of the lost ground, rising to a peak of 468p on the 1st August 1988. The price then fell back before rising again to a peak of 460p on the 8th February 1989. Again the share price failed to make any further progress and fell to its low for the year in December. Following a fall back in the beginning of 1989, the price then recovered gradually before peaking out at 467p on the 24th August. We can now see that since this is within a penny of the peak back in August 1988 we can construct a resistance line at this level, even though 467p or 468p seems to be an odd level for resistance. The line was validated by another attempt at this level on the 28th June 1990, when the price peaked at 467p again.

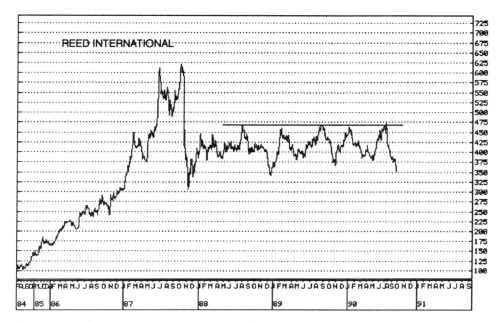

Figure 9.2. A resistance line at 467p in Reed International.

Although the price broke through this line to 472p a few weeks later on the 19th July, this is only 1% above the line, and nothing like the 5% breakthrough that is required to substantiate a failure of the resistance. At the time of writing the price has fallen back to 380p, and another attempt at crossing 467p may be made within the next few months.

The same philosophy of allowing a little tolerance either side of a support or resistance line can be seen in the case of Blue Circle Industries (Figure 9.3). Following a sharp recovery from the crash of 1987, the share price then fell back to 206p on the 8th February 1988 before apparently resuming its upwards move. A week or so later the price came back again to 207p before bouncing upwards again. This time it was three months before the price fell back again, dropping to 208p on the 18th May and staying at that general level until the price inched down to 206p on the 21st June 1988. Another three months later the price was back down to 206p on the 10th September, but then made some progress before running out of steam again and moving back down to 208.5p on the 13th December. This time the price moved upwards consistently, and by the following May was at a peak price of 302p. The price then spent the next five months falling back to the resistance level, reaching 203p on the 27th October 1989. A rally took the price away back up again before dropping back once more. This time the price fell down very slightly through the previously established resistance line, reaching 200p on the 1st May before recovering again. At the time of writing the price had fallen again to 195p on the 23rd August before rising slightly to 208p and then falling to 205p. This failure to rise back rapidly could be a sign that the support level is now turning to a resistance level, but it

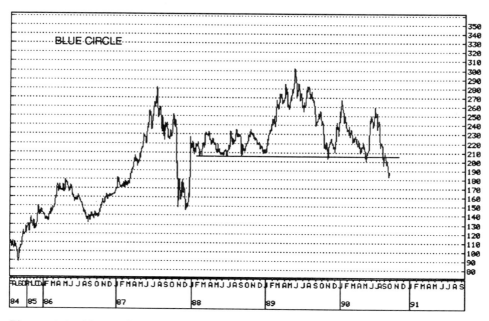

Figure 9.3. More tolerance is needed to draw the Blue Circle resistance line.

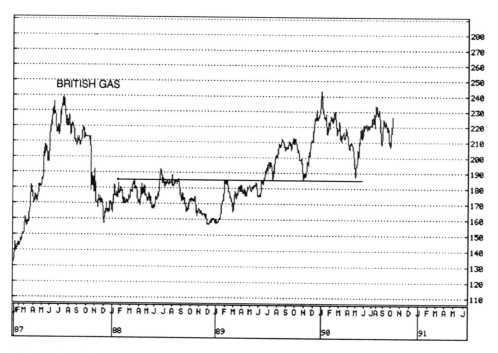

Figure 9.4. A resistance line can become a support line as shown in this example of British Gas.

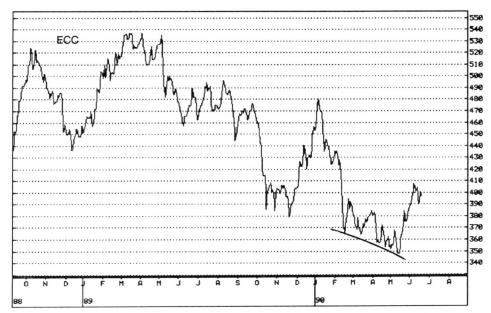

Figure 9.5. A rare example of a curved support line in English China Clays.

is essential that this is confirmed by a fall to 5% below the resistance line. Taking all of the trough prices into account, the resistance line is best drawn at 205p, so as to put all of the troughs into the position of being randomly and, importantly, closely scattered about it. The 5% breakthrough line can therefore be drawn at 195p, a level which has not yet been broken.

It frequently happens that a line can be both a resistance line and a support line, changing from one to the other once the price penetrates through. A good example of this is British Gas, shown in Figure 9.4. The line in question is one that can be drawn at the level of 185p. The price rose to almost this level, 184.5p on the 31st January 1989 before retreating again. The price moved back up to this resistance line again on June 8th, at 184.5p, and then bounced back slightly. Thus the line was established as a resistance line. However, the resistance did not last very long, because by the 19th June the price had passed through it to 186.5p, and then continued up to just below 200p before falling back again. It was at this point that the line became a support line, because the price only fell to 185p before rebounding upwards. This leg of the rise took the price up to nearly 210p over the next few months, but inevitably the price then curved back down again. Once again, upon reaching the line at 185p on the 27th October, the price rose, this time quite sharply, so that a peak price of 243p was reached by the end of December. The price then fell once again, taking four months to arrive back at the region of the support line. This time support was found at 187p and the price rose again quite sharply to just over 230p. At the time of writing the price is well above this support line.

An indication as to its future movement can be obtained by viewing the pattern since mid-1989 as a head and shoulders, the neckline being the support line. Thus symmetry would dictate that we should expect a fall back towards the neckline from the end of August onwards, the 187p mark being reached about the end of October. The line may at that time turn out to be still a support line, with the price rebounding upwards. Investors would be looking out for a completion of the head and shoulders pattern by a fall below this line, so that a further fall could then be anticipated.

Curved support/resistance lines

The vast majority of curved support or resistance lines are simply curved trendlines. For a downtrend a curved line would of course be drawn through the tops of the peaks, so that another way of looking at these would be as curved resistance lines. Conversely for a curved uptrend, a curved line would be drawn through the troughs, and this could be looked at as being a curved support line. However, there are rare occurrences where the curve can be drawn through a set of peaks which fall on an upward curve, or drawn through a set of troughs which fall on a downward curve. Quite clearly, these are neither curved uptrends nor curved downtrends. A beautiful example is shown in Figure 9.5 for English China Clays. Here a series of troughs in the price between October 1989 and May 1990 fall on a downward curve. This formation is not part of a channelled downtrend, because the peaks do not fall on a parallel curve. Although it has not happened yet, a significant (5%) penetration down through this curve would signal a further fall.

Rectangles

A rectangle is an area of congestion of the share price that is limited by both a support line and a resistance line, so that the price spends its time oscillating between the two levels. Since the two lines are parallel to each other, the formation is known as a rectangle. As with normal support and resistance lines, a certain tolerance should be allowed for crossing of these lines, but a 5% crossing is taken to be significant for a continued move in the direction of the penetration.

A recent rectangle that is as yet unresolved can be seen in FIgure 9.6 for Glaxo Holdings. The rectangle can be said to have started in June 1989 with the price at a trough of 666p. The price then rose steadily over the next few months to 812p on the 4th September. It then fell back down again to 671.5p on 24th June 1989 before rising back again to the double peak at 822p and 818p at the end of 1989/beginning of 1990. The price then fell again back to a low of 680p on the 6th March. Once again the price rose from this support level and then spent early 1990 hovering just at the upper resistance line between 821p and 835p. Following a temporary rise above this to 858p, the price then fell back again to 682p on the 23rd August 1990 before recovering again.

The net result of this congestion is that we can draw a lower support line at about 670p and an upper resistance line at 825p. Although the rises and falls of the price do not take it exactly to these levels, it takes it to within 2%. At no time does the price overshoot either of these lines by 5%, and so at the time of writing the price is still confined within the rectangle. As with any rectangle formation, it is not possible to predict whether the

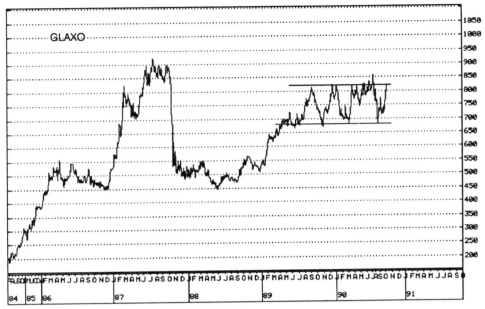

Figure 9.6. An example of a rectangle in the Glaxo share price.

price will break upwards or downwards from this area, it will only be possible to say at the time it happens that a new trend is in progress.

Triangles

There are many forms of triangles, the main types of which are discussed in the following section. Since these formations are so common, it is not necessary to provide more than one example of each type. The crucial aspect of triangles is that a break-out through a side is significant, implying further movement in the same direction, while for triangles other than expanders, there is no significance if the price meanders through to the point. In such a case the future direction of the price cannot be predicted. More often than not, a break-out from a triangle is such that the trend prior to the triangle formation continues, but there are so many examples of opposite behaviour that an investor must wait for the break-out to occur before taking a position.

Since the side of a triangle through which the price breaks out can also be considered to be a trendline, the same criterion must be applied as with trendlines, viz. that a 5% penetration must occur before the penetration is seen as significant.

Expanding Triangles

These are quite rare, and take the form of a cyclic oscillation in the share price growing in amplitude as time goes by. Since they are quite rare, it is not necessary to subdivide them into further categories of right-angles, isosceles, etc. These expanding triangles are

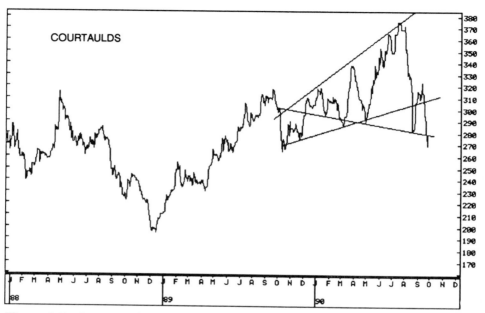

Figure 9.7. An expanding triangle in the Courtaulds share price.

imperfect in the sense that they do not start from a point, but the first oscillation within
their confines is normally quite small. An excellent example of an expander where a
break-out on the downside appears to have just occurred is to be found in the Courtaulds
share price in Figure 9.7. The first trough that can be identified as lying on the lower side
of the triangle is in late 1989, with this side being further defined by two more troughs
in early and mid-1990. The line is sloping gently upwards. The upper side of the triangle
is well defined by a series of peaks during the first half of 1990 that fall on it with almost
perfect precision.

The fall in the Courtaulds share price during the Gulf crisis has taken it much more
than the 5% level below the lower side of the triangle, and therefore the projection is for
a further fall. The usual fall to be predicted is for a similar distance below the lower side
of the triangle as the length of the third side, i.e. the distance between the upper and
lower sides at the time of penetration.

Ascending right-angled triangle

A good example here is the case of Boots just prior to the 1987 crash, as shown in
Figure 9.8. The rising baseline of the triangle is defined by four troughs which show
almost zero scatter about this ideal line. The upper side shows a small amount of scatter
about the ideal horizontal line, but this is extremely small, amounting to less that 2%
either side. As with most formations, it is a penetration by at least 5% that is significant,
and this occurred with the October 1987 fall, which took the price down by almost 30%.

Figure 9.8. An ascending right angled triangle in the Boots share price. The penetration well before the apex is significant.

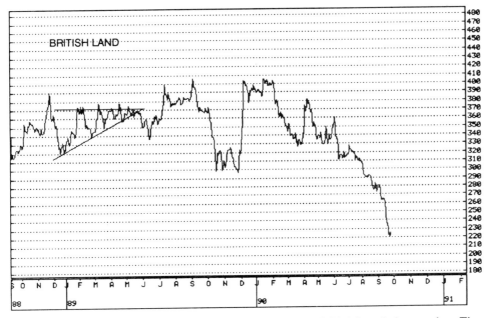

Figure 9.9. An ascending right angled triangle in the British Land share price. The price exits via the apex and the future direction cannot be predicted.

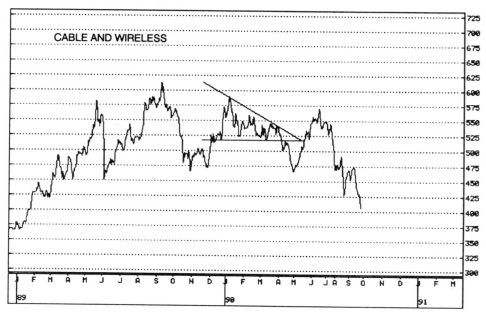

Figure 9.10. A descending right angled triangle in the Cable and Wireless share price. The penetration well before the apex is significant and leads to a price reversal.

As was mentioned above, a price continuation through to the point of the triangle has no significance, and such an example can be found in British Land (Figure 9.9). A right-angled ascending triangle can be drawn during the first half of 1989, and as can be seen, the price did not penetrate the triangle until almost at the apex. Although the price continued downwards, in the direction of the break-out, it did not fall very far before recovering again, confirming the lack of significance of such a late break-out.

Descending right-angled triangle

A short term descending triangle can be seen in the Cable and Wireless share price during the early part of 1990 (Figure 9.10). The oscillations in the price are at their maximum of about 60p at the beginning of the triangle, and these gradually die down to about 10p before the break-out occurs in late March 1990. Here the lower side is horizontal, in contrast to the previous examples. The break-out occurred through this horizontal side which was at a level of 522p. In this case the pattern acts as a reversal pattern, since the uptrend into the triangle is reversed into a downtrend. The fall in the share price took it down to 468p before a temporary recovery took it back up to 570p. The price subsequently fell to 426p by August 1990.

The protection afforded by a 5% penetration requirement can be seen quite clearly in the Sainsbury share price (Figure 9.11). The lower horizontal side of the short term descending triangle formed during late 1989/early 1990 is at 256p, and the price fell down

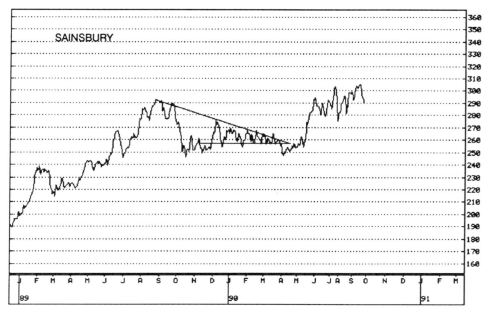

Figure 9.11. A false breakout in this descending right angled triangle in Sainsbury is followed by a significant breakout on the opposite side of the triangle.

through this very sharply to a level of 247p. In view of the short term nature and size of the triangle, this looks a significant break, and many investors would have been tempted to jump the gun. However, this fall was less than 5% down from the base of the triangle, and therefore no action should have been taken. The correctness of this view is confirmed by the price regaining the area of the triangle, and then breaking out sharply on the upside. The price climbed rapidly from 254p on the 11th May to 290p by the 13th June for a useful short term profit.

Isosceles triangle

A good example of an isosceles triangle can be found in the Marks and Spencer share price in the first half of 1988 (Figure 9.12). The line drawn through the tops of the succession of peaks formed during this period slopes downwards, while the line joining the troughs slopes upwards. The slopes of these lines are such that the triangle formed is symmetrical about a horizontal line drawn through the apex, i.e. is isosceles. In this particular case the price broke out of the triangle near the apex to continue with a modest fall from 173p to 152p before recovering back to the level of the apex.

Although a price break-out near to the apex is usually limited in extent, there is sometimes a more dramatic movement. Thus the isosceles triangle formed by the Storehouse share price (Figure 9.13) was such an example. By the end of June 1987 the apex was fast approaching. The price fell slightly to a trough of 284p on the 1st of July and reached the upper side of the triangle with a small rise to 299p on the 14th July. Thus

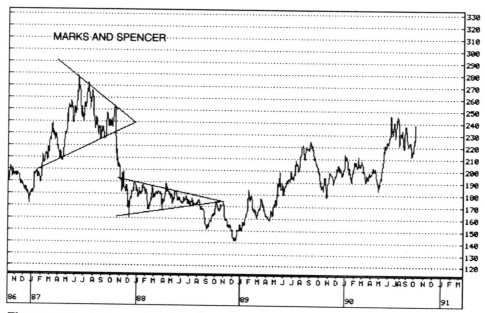

Figure 9.12. An isosceles triangle in Marks and Spencer.

the gap in the triangle is only 15p at this point. The price then rose strongly to gain a third at 390p by August 3rd. The price then made some large oscillations around the 400p level before being caught by the 1987 crash. Interestingly, this is one of the many shares that careful investors would have seen had already passed their best before the crash and would have sold in good time.

Scalene triangle (wedge)

Some writers maintain that the more usual break-out from a wedge formation is in the opposite direction to the way the wedge is pointing, but in this author's experience the break-out is more often such as to reverse the direction of the trend entering the pattern. There are several examples of wedges in the top 100 shares over the last few years, and they all follow this rule. A good example is that of Trafalgar House over 1989 and 1990 (Figure 9.14). The trend at the point of entry into the wedge formation at the end of 1988 was upwards. The wedge is pointing downwards, and the break-out which occurred in July 1990 was downwards, i.e. in the direction of the wedge, but opposite in direction to the trend upon entry. This is a dramatic example, since once the lower side of the wedge was violated, the price fell rapidly by 20% in just a few days.

If further proof is needed of the rule that a wedge formation is usually a reversal formation, then it is doubly provided by Hawker Siddeley, since there are two obvious wedge formations which run into each other, and point in opposite directions. Thus in Figure 9.15 a short term wedge, lasting about six months can be seen for the period at

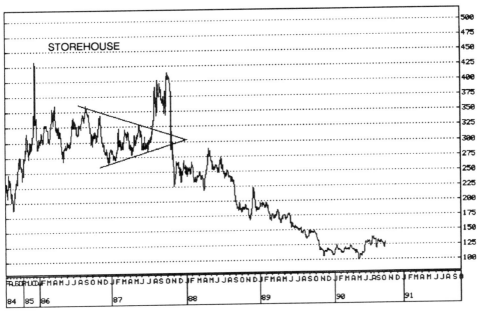

Figure 9.13. An isosceles triangle in Storehouse. The price breakout was caught up by the 1987 crash.

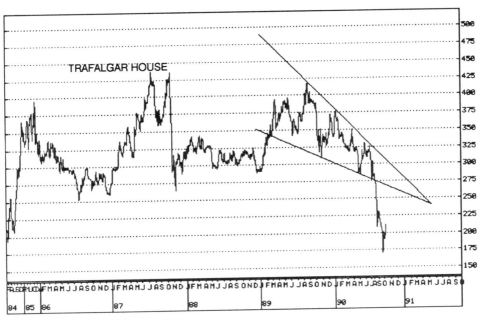

Figure 9.14. A wedge in the Trafalgar House share price. The price breakout is in the opposite direction to the direction of entry.

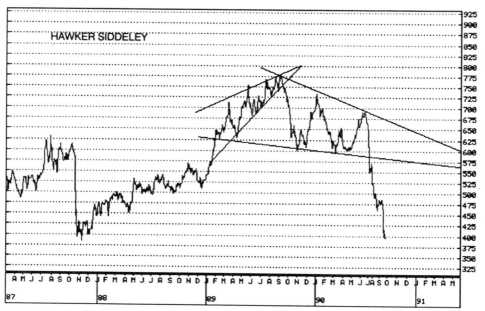

Figure 9.15. There are two wedge formations in the Hawker Siddeley share price. Both act as reversal patterns.

the beginning of 1989. The wedge is pointing upwards, but the break-out was downwards, so as to reverse the trend entering this wedge. This wedge then gives way to a longer term wedge which took over a year from start to break-out. This wedge is pointing downwards, and the break-out was again downwards, again reversing the trend at the start of the wedge in late 1988.

Sometimes a chart is so rich in patterns that it can serve almost as a single example of technical analysis. Thus the case of Ultramar (Figure 9.16) is useful for highlighting several important aspects of charting techniques. First of all a long term ascending triangle formation can be seen which takes about two years for its completion. Next this is a good example of the price leaving the triangle via the apex, where the future price movement is usually indecisive. Note that the upper side of the triangle lies at an horizontal level of 312p. The interesting aspect here is that the upper side of the triangle, as mentioned above, can be considered to be a resistance line, through which the price makes several attempts to penetrate. We have also mentioned that when a resistance line is penetrated it becomes a support level. Not only is this the case here, but the new support level is the base line of another triangle, this time an expander. At the time of writing this latter formation is still in being, and the price has not yet resolved its break-out direction.

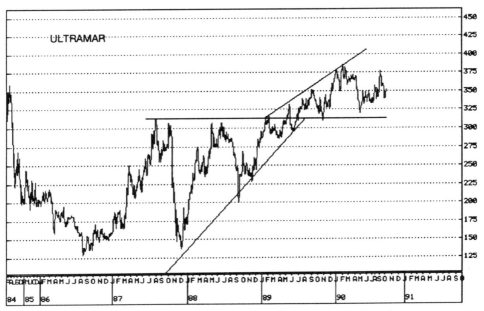

Figure 9.16. Ultramar provides examples of an ascending triangle, an expanding triangle and a line which is both a support and a resistance line.

Flags

Flags are very short term periods of hesitation which follow a rapid rise or rapid fall in the price. They are mini-equivalents of triangles and rectangles, but in the latter case they are more often parallelograms than rectangles. They should last for no more than three weeks before the price resumes its previous direction. Thus they differ from most of the hesitation patterns discussed in that the most likely future direction of the price is known. The extent of the future movement is usually a distance equal to the distance which the price has already moved up or down the flag-pole to the flag. This the flag can be considered to be an area halfway up the flag-pole.

The months of August and September 1990 are rich in falling share prices because of the Gulf crisis, and therefore are also fruitful in providing potential flag formations. At the time of writing many of these have not been resolved. A good example is shown by Allied Irish Bank (Figure 9.17). Here can be seen a definite flag at the end of July 1990, and, true to form, the flag is about halfway down the flag-pole. An interesting aspect of this chart is that August seems to show the formation of another flag, following which the share price made a modest fall before a recovering.

In the case of Reuters (Figure 9.18) the flag is at the same point in time to that of Allied Irish, but the flag is about 300p down the flag-pole, and the price did not fall this amount from the level of the flag. Instead of falling to about 600p, a recovery occurred at 775p, although this may turn out to be short-lived.

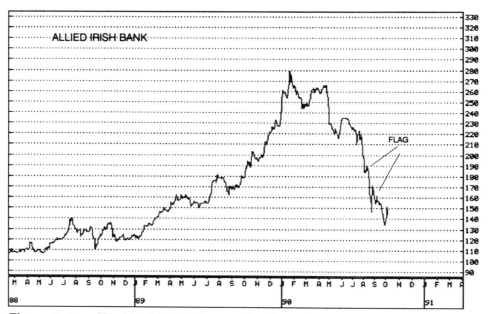

Figure 9.17. Allied Irish Bank shows a flag formation in July 1990 plus another more violent one in August 1990. The first flag is halfway down the "flagpole".

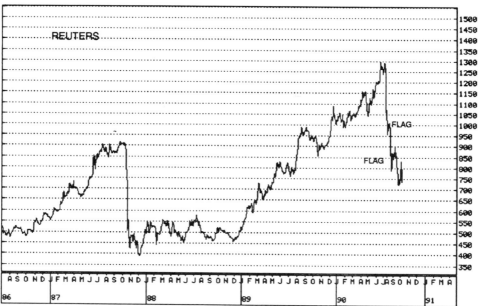

Figure 9.18. Reuters shows similar behaviour to Allied irish Bank. There may even be a third flag in the process of formation.

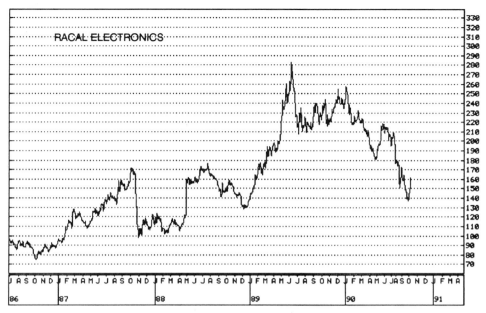

Figure 9.19. An example of an earthquake in Racal Electronics.

Earthquakes

There are quite a few examples of earthquake formations in the top 100 or so shares over the last five years. Such formations are characterised by a sharp fall over no more than a few days, and an equally sharp rise some months or even more than a year later. Where a share has suffered a sharp fall, the investor can therefore be on the look-out for a corresponding rise at a later date. An investor will be unable to capitalise on such a rise as it occurs, because it will occur over one or perhaps two or three days at the most, giving no time to react. The value to the investor is that the extent of the rise is usually equal to the extent of the fall, and while occasionally the rise is a little less than this, it never seems to be greater. A further observation is that over the short term, no further progress tends to be made by the share. Thus an investor should never buy a share which has completed its earthquake formation, and if holding that share, should sell once the share has behaved more quietly for a few days.

A good example of a medium term earthquake can be seen for Racal Electronics between October 1987 and April 1988 (Figure 9.19).

CHAPTER 10

Moving Averages

Moving averages, and the way in which they can be calculated were discussed briefly in Chapter 2. It was also pointed out that moving averages were smoothing devices which removed fluctuations of periodicity equal to or less than the span used for the average. The result of the smoothing process can then be considered to be a "better" representation of the movement of the share price than the actual share price data itself. The greater the span of the average which is used, the smoother is the resulting plot.

A good example to illustrate the effect of various moving averages is the chart of the Allied Lyons share price, a history from the beginning of 1984 being shown in Figure 10.1. It is a good example because of the large amount of cyclic movement which is obviously present. The horizontal grids have been left out of the charts in this chapter in order to present a clearer picture of the moving average curves.

A commonly used moving average is one of 200 days, and this is used to isolate the underlying longer term trends in a share price history. As was mentioned above, an average removes fluctuations of periodicity less than or equal to than the span of the average. Thus we would expect a 200 day moving average to remove cycles of wavelength of 200 days or less. Looking again at the chart in Figure 10.1,we can see that the cycles which are in evidence for the period since early 1988 have trough to trough or peak to peak distances which are about half a year or less, i.e. their wavelengths are half a year, about 120 business days. Thus on the basis of what we have just said, we would expect these to be removed by a 200 day average. On the other hand, the large cyclical movement which had as its final trough the time of the 1987 crash had its earlier trough over a year previously, i.e. a wavelength of perhaps 300 days or more. Thus we would not expect this cycle to be removed by a 200 day average.

That this approach is correct can be seen by the shape of the 200 day average of the Allied Lyons share price which is illustrated in Figure 10.2. As predicted, the cycles which were visible since 1988 have been removed, but the cycle which ended with the 1987 crash can be seen.

By the same argument, the use of a shorter span moving average such as 20 days would result in the removal of cycles of 20 days or less wavelength. Since the cycles which are present since 1988 have wavelengths of about 120 days, we would not expect these to be removed by such an average, although we would expect to lose the random day to day movement and any cycles which have very short wavelengths of less than 20 days. That this does indeed happen can be seen quite clearly from the plot of the 20 day moving average of the Allied Lyons share price in Figure 10.3.

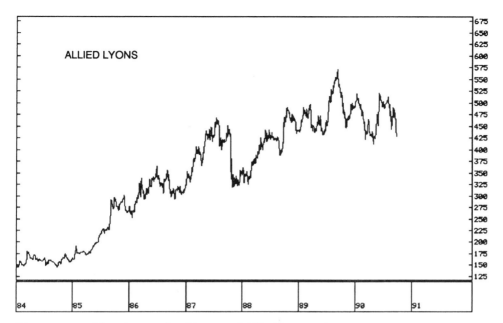

Figure 10.1. The share price history of Allied Lyons since 1984.

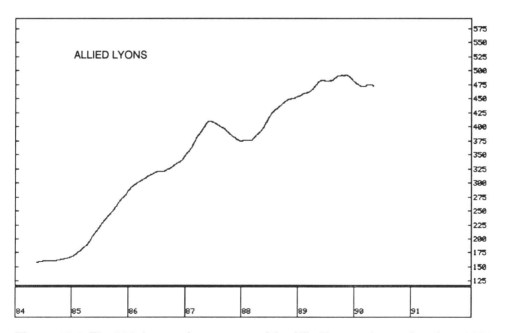

Figure 10.2. The 200 day moving average of the Allied Lyons share price since 1984.

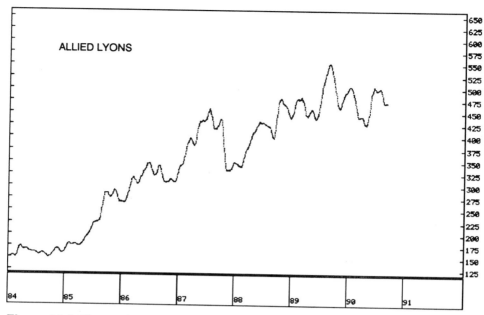

Figure 10.3. The 20 day moving average of the Allied Lyons share price since 1984.

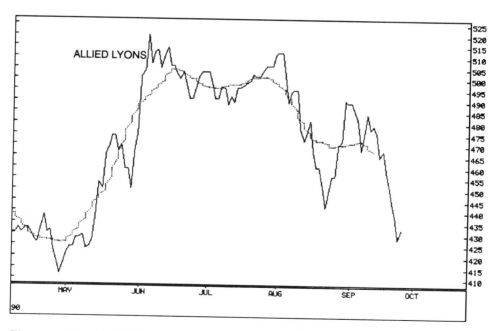

Figure 10.4. The 20 day moving average and the Allied Lyons share price since April 1990. The average is plotted half a span back in time so as to show that the average is a smoother version of the price itself.

In order to get a clear idea of the smoothing effect of a moving average, the final few months of the Allied Lyons share price is shown in Figure 10.4 with the 20 day average superimposed. In this case, in order to preserve the relationship between the data and the average, the average has been offset half a span back in time. In this mode of plotting, the average is directly superimposable upon the data (see chapter on Channel Analysis). It can now be seen that the average is the best smooth line drawn through the data so that the very short term fluctuations are removed.

These few examples should serve to put into perspective the reasons for selecting particular spans. For the trader interested in short term movements, it is essential that cycles of short wavelength are not removed from the data. Thus a short span average, for example of 10 days up to 50 days must be used in order to preserve such cycles while removing the day to day variations. On the other hand, the longer term investor is more interested in the long term underlying trends and not in the shorter term trends. Thus these short term trends can be removed and the longer term trends highlighted by selecting an average such as 200 or 240 days.

Moving average applications

There are almost as many ways of applying moving averages as there are investors who use them. The three main methods are:

- Buying and selling when the share price crosses the moving average.
- Buying and selling when one moving average crosses another.
- Buying and selling when a moving average changes direction.
- Using an average to give the current state of an underlying trend, usually long term.

Price crossing a single average

In this method, as in all other methods discussed in this chapter, moving averages are plotted with no lag, i.e. the latest calculated point is plotted on the time axis at the same place in time as the latest data point used to calculate it. Thus the average and the data will always end at the same point in time.

The signal to buy is when the share price, which will have been running below the smoother average line, crosses up through this line, and conversely, the time to buy will be when the price falls down through the average line. Some investors will use this method only for generating a buying signal and do not use it for selling. They will use methods such as a stop loss in order to secure the profit from the rising share price or to terminate a trade which fails to generate a profit in the first place.

A derivative of this price crossing method is to use two averages. The second, longer span average is not used in conjunction with crossing by the share price, but used to modify the buying or selling decision generated by crossing of the first average. Thus a share will only be bought when a buying signal is generated if this second average is in a rising mode, and a share will not be sold if this longer term average is in a falling mode. This second average therefore comes under the fourth category above, where it is used solely to give an indication of the underlying trend. Used in this way, this will naturally

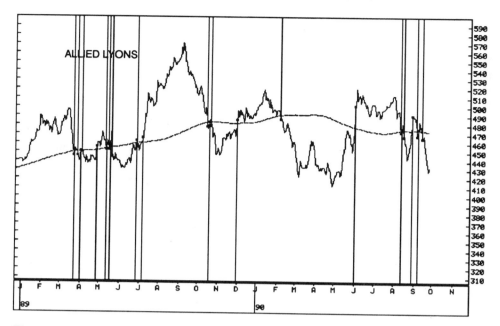

Figure 10.5. The 200 day moving average and the Allied Lyons share price since 1984.

reduce the number of buying and selling opportunities compared with the use of just a single average.

The only decision which has to be made with the single average method is the span to be used for the moving average. While as we have stated a 200 day moving average will leave only the long term trends visible, we will find that such an average is unsuitable for the method because of the time lag associated with it. Being much smoother than a short term average, it is much slower to respond to a rise or fall in share price than a short term average. This fact can be demonstrated by two examples, one in which a crossing of the 200 day average is used as a buying or selling signal, and one in which a crossing of a 50 day average is used for the signals.

In Figure 10.5 is shown the share price of Allied Lyons since the beginning of 1989, and superimposed upon this is a 200 day moving average. The vertical lines below the average indicate points where the price broke up through the average, i.e. generated buying signals. The vertical lines above the average indicate points where the price fell down through the average, i.e. generated selling signals. Thus we can see that during the period in question there were 13 buying signals and 14 selling signals. Of the 13 pairs of buying/selling transactions, 12 gave a selling signal at a price lower than the previous buying signal, i.e. the investor would have lost money in all but one transaction. Thus quite obviously a 200 day average is far too unresponsive for such a method to succeed.

In Figure 10.6 is shown a similar chart but with the average now reduced in span to one of 50 days. This time there are only 8 complete transactions. This time they are split

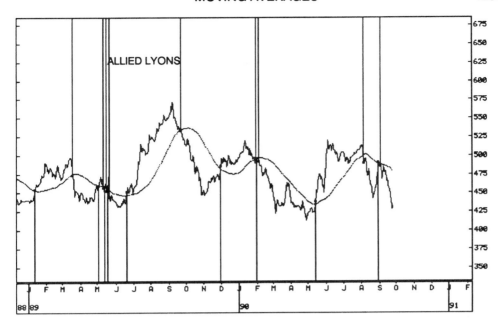

Figure 10.6. The 50 day moving average and the Allied Lyons share price since 1984.

as 4 losers and 4 winners. Thus it has been an advantage to move the span of the average to shorter periods. Notice also that in comparing buying signals between the two Figures by means of the vertical lines in Figure 10.6 that the signals are considerably earlier.

It might appear that it would be an advantage to move to even shorter averages, such as 20 day or 10 day. The problem in doing this is that the number of false signals, i.e. those occasions where the price crosses the average only to recross it in the opposite direction a few days later increases dramatically. Such situations obviously lead to losses. This leads to the conclusion that a little research has to be done to determine the optimum average for a particular share. With a computer system this is an easy task, but if averages are calculated manually, then it is daunting to compute say ten different averages for one share. It will usually be found to be the case that an average somewhere between 30 and 50 days will give the best results, i.e. the greatest overall gain. In order to get an appreciation of the price movement that occurs between buying and selling signals, the dates of the buying and selling signals and the share prices at those dates for the 50 day average in the case of Allied Lyons are shown in Table 10.1. These of course correspond to the signals shown in Figure 10.6.

Note that the four losing situations give only small losses, while the winning situations give larger gains. If dealing costs are ignored the percentage gain over the eight transactions is 27%. If dealing costs are applied to the figures, then the investor would have come out with a very small profit.

Table 10.1. The dates and prices for buying and selling signals generated by the Allied Lyons share price crossing the 50 day average.

Date	Buying price	Date	Selling price	200 day average
13/01/89	458	17/03/89	473	Rising
04/05/89	464	10/05/89	456	Rising
15/05/89	462	16/05/89	452	Rising
18/05/89	457	22/05/89	444	Rising
21/06/89	451	22/09/89	531	Rising
30/11/89	485	30/01/90	490	Falling
31/01/90	495	05/02/90	491	Falling
04/05/90	438	06/08/90	489	Falling

In the last column of Table 10.1 is shown the status of the 200 day average. As mentioned above, the status of such a long term average is often used as a modifier to the buying or selling signal. As a buying modifier, it is used to confirm a buy if it is rising, but negate a buy if it is falling. The opposite view is taken for selling decisions, although it is unusual to use this method for other than buying decisions. As can be seen from Table 10.1, used in this way only four buying decisions would have been made, two winners and two losers.

The Allied Lyons case was chosen particularly to illustrate situations where the use of the average crossing method is not very successful and to show why this is the case. This approach is a necessary one, since an investor should always be aware of the reasons for a method failing in order to be able to correct for it. The Allied Lyons situation, with its very cyclical behaviour over the past two years has offered, at least theoretically, good profit making prospects for investors who could time the buying and selling decisions correctly. The cycles have given price rises of between 20% and 30%.

The reason for the poor performance of the method in the Allied Lyons case is simple. It is because the price rose rapidly from the troughs and fell back rapidly from the peaks. With a rapid rise, the price overshoots the rising average by a large amount, thereby limiting the proportion of the rise which is captured by the investor. At the other end of the transaction, a rapid fall has the same effect, the price having fallen a considerable distance from the peak before the selling decision is triggered. As was mentioned above, although the obvious fix for this problem would seem to lie with a reduction in the span of the average, so that the average begins to rise or fall much sooner, this is negated by an increase in the number of false signals.

Where the average crossing method does score is in those situations where the share price has tended to follow gentler but more sustained rises. In these cases the price crosses the average at a much more reasonable rate so that the investor is not faced with a large gap between the average and the price at the time of the buying signal. A good example of such a successful application of the crossing method is shown by the share price of Reuters where a 200 day average is superimposed (Figure 10.7). Here we have

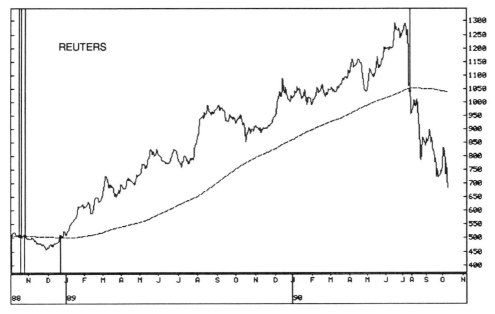

Figure 10.7. The price crossings of the 200 day average for the Reuters share price. The sustained rise in the share price kept the number of crossings down to two.

a sustained rise in price through 1989 and the first half of 1990, and the price only crosses the average on two occasions. The buying signal is given on the 20th December 1988 at a price of 503p and the selling signal on the 3rd August 1990 at 1039p for a gain of 106%.

Note though the comparative failure of the method from the selling point of view. The price fell from just below 1300p to 1039p before the selling signal was triggered. Again, the average is unable to deal with the rapid rate of price change at this point in time. Note also that at the extreme left hand side of the Figure there are three selling points and two buying points over the course of just a few days. This happens because the average is almost horizontal at that point, and the normal random day to day price movements cause the price to cross and recross the average repeatedly.

The general conclusion from this discussion of the average crossing method is that although it is widely used, a great deal of research is required to find the best average for a particular share, and even then, the results over a long period are not particularly startling.

Two averages crossing

As was pointed out above, one difficulty with the price/average crossing method is that fairly short term fluctuations in the share price can take it above and below the average repeatedly, giving false signals which lose the investor money. One way around this is to use the crossing of two averages. The shorter term average is used as a substitute for the price, and since it will now be smoother than the price fluctuations, there should be fewer false signals given. The penalty for this improvement will be that the shorter term average

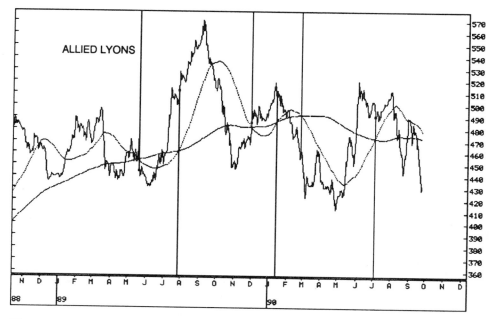

Figure 10.8. Buying and selling signals generated by crossing of the 50 day and 200 day moving averages of the Allied Lyons share price.

will have lost some speed of response when compared with the price itself, and therefore there will be a longer lag time until the signal is given. This will reduce the effective gain which can be made from the transaction. As with all stock market investment, what we have is a method of reducing the risk which will always result in a reduced return.

As a start, we can take two averages which are fairly widely spaced. Thus a 200 day average will give a good indication of the longer term trend, and a 50 day average should give a reasonably smooth crossing average. Figure 10.8 shows that the number of buying and selling signals is now sharply reduced to three complete transactions. If the first buying signal on the 28th July is examined more closely, it will be seen that it lags well behind the points at which the price crosses the 50 day average and then the 200 day average. This delay is so serious that the price has risen to 528p on the 28th July before the signal is given. For the corresponding selling point, this is not given until the 30th November 1989, when the price is down to 485p. Thus although the share price showed an excellent rise between June and September 1989, this method resulted in a loss. Thus the averages employed were of far too long a span to give any sensitivity to the price rise and fall.

Moving to shorter term averages, in Figure 10.9 is shown the effect of using a 10 day average and a 50 day average. Taking the June to September cycle first, it can be seen that the buying point occurs much further back in time, occurring on the 28th June 1989 when the price was 462p. The selling point was also moved back to a point nearer to the peak price, occurring on the 27th September at 522p. The overall gain for the five complete transactions during the period of the chart was just under 5%. This is now

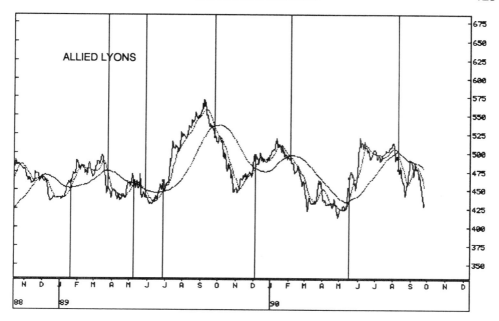

Figure 10.9. Buying and selling signals generated by crossing of the 10 day and 50 day moving averages of the Allied Lyons share price.

inferior to the 27% obtained by the price/average crossing method. However, the two averages crossing method can be improved dramatically by one simple rule. Only buy at a crossing point if both averages are rising. Such crossing points have been called 'Golden Crosses'. Their effect in the Allied Lyons case is to rule out three of the five transactions. The first allowable transaction was the one mentioned above, buying at 462p and selling at 522p, a gain of 13%, while the second one was buying at 466p on the 17th May 1990 and selling at 472p on the 13th August 1990 for a gain of 1.3%. The compound gain from these two transactions, i.e. investing the proceeds of the first transaction into the second is 14.4%, ignoring dealing costs. If dealing costs are taken into consideration then the gain would be of the order of 6 to 7%.

Comparing this result to that for the price crossing method, we can see that because the number of transactions is greatly reduced then the dealing costs are much less. Taking dealing costs into account the profit from the price crossing of the 50 day average was just about zero, while the profit for this current method was between 6 and 7%. Superficially the Golden Cross method does seem to be superior. It must be emphasised however, that each share behaves differently, and a true comparison of any methods can only be made with a great deal of effort across a large number of shares.

Change in direction of an average

· The principle behind this method is that moving averages isolate trends. The type of trend being isolated, i.e. whether it is short, medium or long term depends entirely upon the span of the average being used. Once an average changes direction, then the trends of longer periodicity than the span of the average have also changed direction. How long they remain running in the new direction cannot be determined, since a subsequent reversal of direction will depend upon random factors. It is sufficient to know that the end of a trend will be signalled in exactly the same way as its beginning, viz by a change in the direction of the appropriate moving average.

As with any other moving average method, the crucial factor is the span used for the average which is being used as an indicator. Large spans will isolate long term trends, but the delay in a change of direction of the average will mean that a considerable portion of the ensuing price rise or price fall will have already occurred. In the book 'Stocks and Shares Simplified' the use of two averages was advocated, a 5 week (25 day) average for those investors who wished to take advantage of very short term trends and a 13 week (65 day) average for those investors who had longer term ambitions. It was also pointed out that while the shorter average captured more of the gain, it also gave more false signals.

As an example, a plot of Allied Lyons with the 25 day average is shown in Figure 10.10. The turning points in the average are marked by vertical lines, those at the top half being the selling signals, and those in the bottom half the buying signals. There are thirteen possible complete transactions, and these are listed in Table 10.2. The overall percentage gain for these transactions was just under 23%. Thus in the case of Allied Lyons the method is broadly comparable with the first method of price crossing.

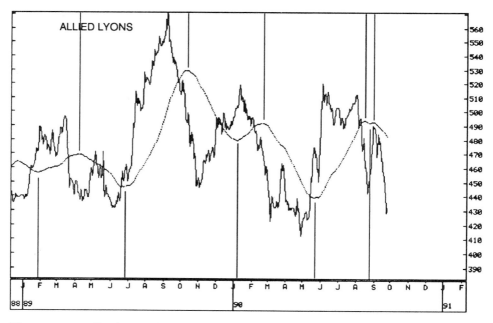

Figure 10.10. Buying and selling signals generated by change in direction of the 25 day moving average of the Allied Lyons share price.

Table 10.2. Buying and selling points in the Allied Lyons share price as signalled by changes in the direction of the 25 day average.

Date	Buying price	Date	Selling price
19/01/89	461	27/02/89	467
02/03/89	475	06/03/89	481.5
08/03/89	488	17/03/89	473
28/04/89	459	24/05/89	442
25/05/89	447	26/05/89	441
22/06/89	457	23/06/89	451
27/06/89	457	21/09/89	533
28/11/89	467	05/02/90	491
09/04/90	430	11/04/90	430
20/04/90	438	23/04/90	430
14/05/90	438	10/07/90	488
31/07/90	511	03/08/90	501
07/08/90	494	08/08/90	495

This author has always held the view that taken across a large number of shares, the average turning point method is superior to the other moving average methods discussed here because of its more fundamental nature. It is focusing attention on the behaviour of trends and especially on their turning points. It will be most successful for those shares in which trends persist for the longest, and these shares can be discovered by simple inspection of their moving averages to pin-point those which have the fewest turning points over their price history for a given average such as 25 days or 65 days.

A useful comparison between the three methods discussed is carried out in Table 10.3 for the first 10 shares in the top 100 list for the period 1st January 1989 to the end of September 1990.

The use of the turning point of the average can now be seen to be superior in these cases, although the use of the method of the price crossing a 50 day average is not far behind. Of the three methods, the use of two averages crossing gives a substantially lower return.

Use of averages to show underlying long term trend

This method of using averages is a useful adjunct to the confirmation of reversal patterns. Many commercial chart services show a price history with a 200 day or 240 day average superimposed. As we discussed earlier, such an average is of little use by itself as a buying or selling indicator, but it is extremely useful as an indicator of the direction of the underlying trend. Thus in Chapter 6 it was pointed out that it is sometimes difficult to confirm that a double bottom formation has been completed until some considerable time after the price is on its way up from the second leg of the formation. As can be seen from the chart of Shell in Figure 10.11, the fact that the 200 day moving average has

Table 10.3. A comparison of the gains made in the first 10 of the top 100 shares since the 1st January 1989 by each of the three moving average methods. Price/average is the crossing of the price and the 50 day average. Average /average is the crossing of the 10 day and 50 day averages. Average turn is the change in direction of the 25 day average.

Security	Price/Average	Average/average	Average turn
Abbey National	32.14	13.1	34.33
Assoc British Foods	19.05	17.17	30.62
Allied Lyons	27.08	4.92	22.96
Amstrad -	2.85	-21.22	0.42
Argyll	27.28	31.34	13.00
Asda	32.93	31.78	15.58
BAA	19.98	30.09	20.88
British Airways	5.73 -	23.78	21.17
Barclays	16.99	-0.95	38.26
Bass	27.12	34.61	44.89
Average gains	20.54	11.77	24.21

Figure 10.11. The 200 day moving average of the Shell share price is helpful in deciding whether a bottoming formation is complete..

started to move upwards is useful confirmatory evidence that the double bottom formation has been completed.

There are many such cases of ambiguity which can be assisted by the use of a long term moving average, and the investor is encouraged to use them whenever possible for this purpose.

CHAPTER 11

RELATIVE STRENGTH AND MOMENTUM

In 'Stocks and Shares Simplified' it was pointed out that a knowledge of general market conditions was essential to the making of buying and selling decisions for specific shares. When the general trend of the market is downwards the reasons for buying a particular share must be overpowering, since sooner or later most shares get caught up in the ebb tide. The performance of a share relative to the market in general is thus an important yardstick. Fortunately we have available to us a simple but powerful means of measuring this relative performance in the Relative Strength Indicator.

Another useful piece of information about a share is the head of steam that has been built up behind a rise; this is best interpreted by the concept of momentum. There are several indicators which measure momentum, and the Welles Wilder Index is probably the most popular.

Relative Strength Index (RSI)

The Relative Strength Indicator is simple if laborious to calculate. It is simply the ratio of the share price to a broadly based index such as the All Share Index or the FTSE100 Index calculated from day to day. The RSI is then plotted on the same chart as the share price. Although the values for the RSI will be quite different from those for the share price, the values are scaled so that the RSI can be plotted on the same chart, usually either below or above the share price. The actual values for the RSI are unimportant, so that the scale for these can be omitted from the plot. This is not done in the examples here because the RSI has been plotted in a separate box in order to enlarge the trends for easier reading.

As an example to get an idea of the appearance of an RSI, this index is plotted, along with the share price for Allied Lyons from late 1988 in Figure 11.1. It can be seen that although there are some similarities between the RSI in the lower box and the share price in the upper box, there are also many differences. When the RSI is increasing, this means that the share price is outperforming the market, while when it is decreasing, the share price is underperforming the market. Thus in Figure 11.1, the RSI decreases steadily during the first seven months, showing that Allied Lyons is underperforming the market. The situation is rectified by the rise from June 1989 until September 1989, and then the performance drops off once again.

While these rises and falls in the share performance are interesting, they are not terribly helpful in themselves. It is the application of charting techniques, especially the use of trendlines, that makes the RSI a powerful tool for the determination or confirmation of buying and selling points. Such a trendline has been drawn on the RSI

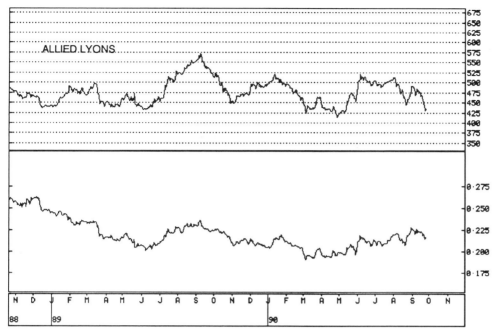

Figure 11.1. The Allied Lyons share price (upper panel) with the Relative Strngth Index (lower panel). The latter uses the FTSE100 Index as the base.

in Figure 11.2. Since, as mentioned above, the RSI shows a lengthy downtrend until mid-1989, it is useful to see whether the end of this downtrend can be established by means of penetration of the trendline as was the case with share prices. It can be seen from Figure 11.2 that this is indeed the case. There are three peaks which lie on the downtrend line. The point at which the RSI moves up through this line, hence breaking the trend, is shown by the vertical line. The date corresponding to this point is the 27th June 1989 with the price at 457p. Note that this is the same date that the signal was given by a change in direction of the 25-day average (Chapter 10).Thus the use of a trendline with the RSI appears, at least in this case, to be a useful indicator.

It was mentioned earlier that the more difficult cases for an investor are the single bottoming and topping formations, since early in their development they could be the beginning of many other patterns such as inverted head and shoulders, triple tops, etc. It is therefore instructive to see if the RSI can be of use in these situations.

In Figure 11.3 is shown the chart of Rolls-Royce, the topping formation in which was discussed in Chapter 7 (Figure 7.3). It was difficult to know when to sell this share because it had a rounded top and because there were numerous short term fluctuations superimposed on it. In the lower panel the RSI is shown, and a trendline is drawn through the peaks on the uptrend from the beginning of 1989. The RSI penetrated this uptrend line on the 13th June 1989, thus giving a selling signal. The price at that point was 188.5p. Considering the peak price of 197.5p was passed only a month previously on the 19th

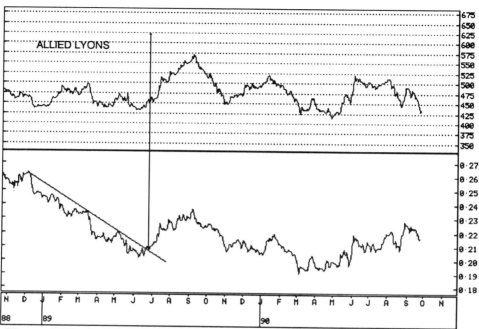

Figure 11.2. A downtrend line is now drawn on the RSI chart for the first part of 1989. The downtrend is broken on 27th June 1989 as marked by the vertical line.

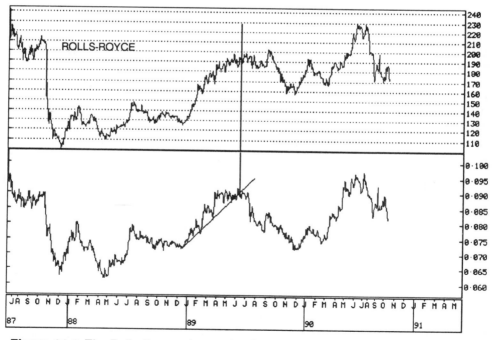

Figure 11.3. The Rolls-Royce share price (upper panel) with the Relative Strength Index (lower panel). The latter uses the FTSE100 Index as the base. A trendline is drawn.

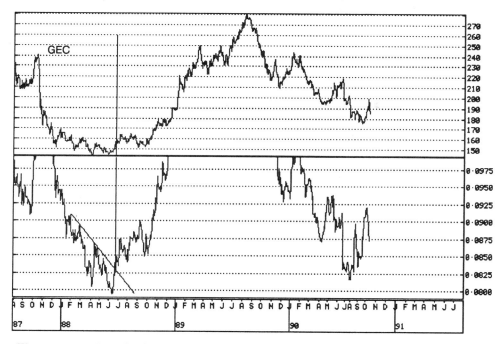

Figure 11.4. The GEC share price (upper pane) with the RSI (lower panel).

May, this is a very good example of the usefulness of the RSI method. The selling point was only 4.5% down from the peak price. The price rebounded slightly after this selling point to reach 198.5p on the 27th June, but realistically only luck would have got an investor out at this price.

As an example of a rounded bottoming formation, the chart of GEC (Figure 11.4) has already been discussed in Chapter 6 (Figure 6.1).The rounded bottoming formation started in late 1987 and took almost the whole of 1988 to complete. The advantage of using the RSI method of determining a buying point is shown in the lower panel of Figure 11.4. In order to show the fine detail so that a trendline could be drawn the plot has been magnified vertically. Although this takes the central portion off the top of the scale this does not matter for this exercise.We can now see that there are three obvious peaks present at the beginning of 1988 that enable a valid trendline to be drawn. The RSI surged up through this trendline on the 23rd June 1988, as shown by the position marked by the vertical line. The price at that point was 155p. The lowest point reached by the share price was 143p on the 6th April, so this buying point was within 8.4% of the lowest price. After a brief rise the price dipped back again, but only to 153.5p on the 30th August, so that the investor was never substantially in deficit from this buying time onwards. A substantial gain was made in the following twelve months, since the price maintained its upwards momentum, reaching 280p by the middle of 1989 for a substantial profit. These few examples should serve to show the potential for the RSI method. Just as with the other indicators discussed in this book, there will be failures as well as successes, but the RSI has stood the test of time and is a useful addition to the range of indicators available to the investor.

The Welles Wilder Index (WWI)

This is one of several indicators which measure the momentum of a share price movement. As was shown in Chapter 2 where its calculation was outlined, it results in a value which always lies between zero and one hundred. The general consensus is that when the value falls below 30, the share in question is oversold, and can be bought, while if the value rises above 70 the share is overbought and should therefore be sold. Although any period can be used as the basis of the calculation, the accepted one is a 14 day period, and all the examples that follow use this value. A few examples here will serve to show circumstances in which the indicator has turned out to be useful.

The chart of the Barclays share price with the 14-day WWI is shown in Figure 11.5. It can be seen that there is quite a good correlation between peaks and troughs in the share price and the points at which the WWI crosses the 70 and 30 levels.

There are several methods of using the WWI to generate buying and selling signals. Some investors use the method of buying or selling on an immediate cross of these levels.

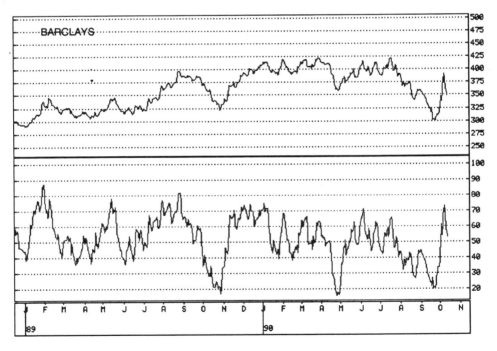

Figure 11.5. The Barclays share price (upper panel) with the Welles Wilder Index (lower panel).

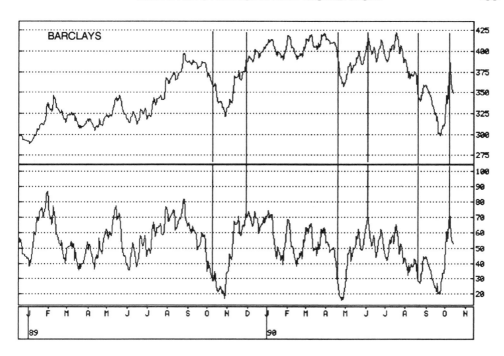

Figure 11.6. The Barclays share price (upper panel) with the Welles-Wilder Index (lower panel). The vertical lines show the points where the Index crosses the 30 and 70 levels.

Table 11.1. The dates and prices for the buying and selling operations in Barclays as signalled by the WW Index crossing the 30 and 70 levels.

Date	Buy at	Date	Sell at	% Gain
10/10/89	357	30/11/89	387	8.4
19/04/90	388	05/06/90	416	7.2
21/08/90	344	08/10/90	390	13.4

Others wait until the WWI has troughed if falling below 30 or peaked if rising above 70. Yet others wait for a recrossing of the level in the opposite direction before taking action.

The results of applying this first method, i.e. buying or selling on an initial crossing of the 30 and 70 lines, to Barclays shares from the end of 1988 is shown in Figure 11.6. The points at which the WWI crosses the 30 or 70 levels are marked by vertical lines so that the corresponding point on the share price chart can be seen. Now that the chart scale has been enlarged, a very important property of the WWI can now be seen: the buying and selling signals usually occur before the turning point in the share price. This is quite

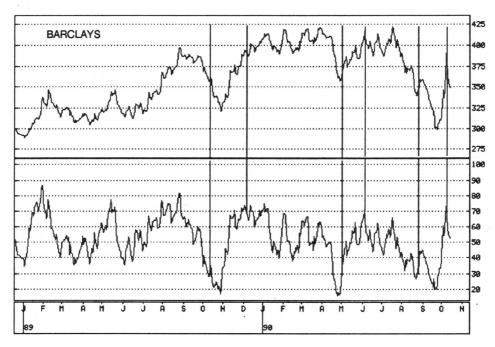

Figure 11.7. The Barclays share price (upper panel) with the Welles Wilder Index (lower panel). The vertical linesshow the points where the Index recrosses the 30 and 70 levels.

marked for the trough in the Barclays price that occurred at the end of October 1989. The buying signal given by a crossing of the 30 line by the WWI occurred on the 10th October, when the price was 357p. The actual trough in the share price occurred on the 27th October 1989 when the price was 320p. The dates and corresponding share prices for the three complete buying and selling operations shown by the vertical lines in Figure 11.6 are listed in Table 11.1.

The average gain from the three transactions is 9.7%. This can be compared with the gain made by using the alternative method of buying and selling when the price crosses back up through the 30 level and back down through the 70 level. These points are shown in the chart in Figure 11.7. The dates and prices for these buying and selling operations are shown in Table 11.2. Now the average gain from the three transactions is 9.0%. This is so close to the value from using the first method that it has to be said that there is no significant difference between the two methods, at least in the case of the Barclays share price.

It is of interest to see how well the WWI performs for the difficult cases of rounded bottoms and rounded tops, mentioned earlier in this chapter. The chart of GEC, with the WWI in the lower panel, is shown in Figure 11.8. It can be seen quite clearly that the WWI fell below the 30 level in October 1987 at the time of the crash. This point is obviously about eight months prior to the lowest point reached in the share price during

Table 11.2. The dates and prices for the buying and selling operations in Barclays as signalled by the WW Index recrossing the 30 and 70 levels.

Date	Buy at	Date	Sell at	% Gain
12/10/89	360	07/12/89	390	8.3
02/05/90	371	06/06/90	409	10.2
27/08/90	346	09/10/90	375	8.4

the following year. Moreover, the share price at the time of the crossing of the 30 level was considerably higher than the low price reached in the middle of 1988. Thus, an investor who used the WWI buying signal for GEC would have seen a steady deterioration in the share price. In the case of the topping formation in Rolls-Royce, the charts in Figure 11.9 show that the WWI crossed the 70 level at the end of December 1988 when the share price was only halfway back up to its highest point of 200p during the topping pattern. Thus, again in such a difficult case, the WWI gets the investor in out too soon. There is no intention here to leave the investor with a totally negative feeling for the WWI, but rather to leave the investor being cautious about acting on the basis of the WWI alone. Just to show that the WWI can often get an investor in very close to the bottom price. The Boots share price is a very good example. As shown in Figure 11.10,

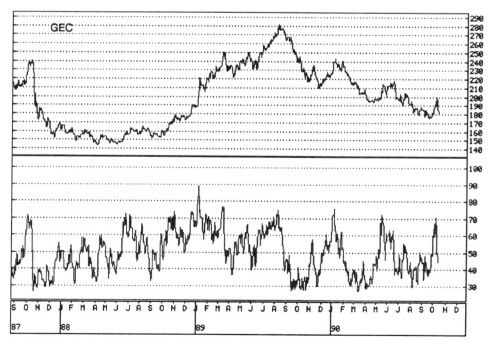

Figure 11.8. The chart of the GEC share price (upper panel) with the WW Index (lower panel).

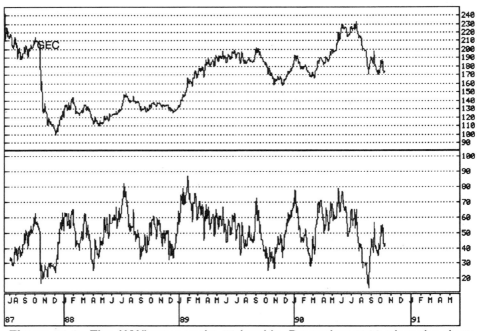

Figure 11.9. The WWI crosses the 70 level in December 1988 when the share price is only halfway up to its peak.

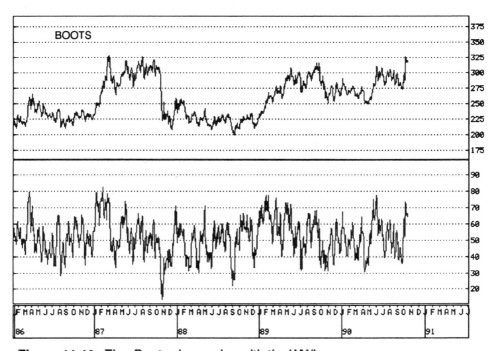

Figure 11.10. The Boots share price with the WWI.

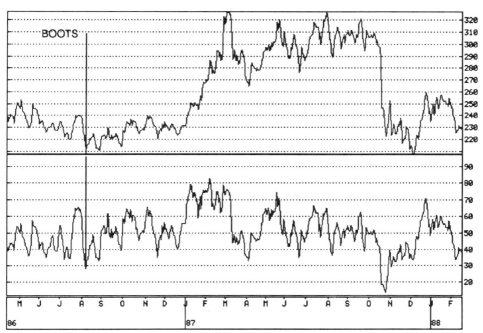

Figure 11.11. The Boots share price and the WWI. The price scale is magnified to show the buying signal in August 1986.

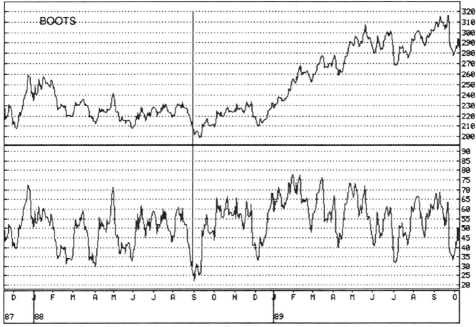

Figure 11.12. The buying signal for Boots shares generated in August 1988 by the WW Index falling below 30.

it can be seen that there are two areas of a low price below 210p which were followed by useful rises to above 310p. Thus the success or otherwise of the WWI in getting an investor into Boots in these low price areas is an important consideration. In Figure 11.11, the share price scale is magnified so as to show more clearly the behaviour of both the share price and the WWI from June 1986 to the end of 1987. The WW Index fell below the 30 level on the 7th August 1986. This was exactly at the actual trough, which was at a price level of 211p. Thus the WWI got the investor in at exactly the lowest price. From this point of view the WWI can be said to have been extremely successful. Another such opportunity occurred in 1988, and this portion of the chart is shown in enlarged view in Figure 11.12. Here the vertical line shows that the WWI fell below the 30 level on the 30th August 1988, when the price was 207p. The price continued to fall for a few days more before bottoming out at 199p on the 8th September. Thus once again the WWI got the investor in very close to the bottom price, within 3.5%.

The examples presented here serve to show the usefulness of the Welles Wilder Index, and since it gives advance warning of the possibility of a trough or peak in the share price, it can be used even more successfully in conjunction with the other indicators discussed in these chapters.

CHAPTER 12

THE RISE-FALL INDICATOR

I first wrote about this indicator in 'Stocks and Shares Simplified', where it was shown to be excellent for getting investors in and out of shares close to the major troughs and peaks. It has been left out of later books for one reason only, and that is because of the great difficulty in programming it into a computer so as to generate the type of automatic buy and sell signals which are so readily produced by moving averages and other numerical indicators such as the Welles Wilder Index. The Rise-Fall Indicator (RFI) depends upon the breaking of trendlines, and therefore is entirely appropriate to a book such as this which is devoted to charting techniques.

The way in which the RFI is produced was discussed in Chapter 2. The previous value of the indicator is increased by one if the share price rises, is decreased by one if the share price falls, and stays unchanged if the share price is unchanged. The initial starting value for the indicator is set at some round number such as 100. From such a start it is extremely unlikely that the indicator will fall to anything approaching zero since to do this the share price would have to suffer one hundred more falls than rises in the period in question. Even if it did fall to zero this does not effect the interpretation of the indicator.

Because the RFI is only concerned with whether a share price has fallen, risen or stayed still, and not with the actual price movement itself, it can be considered to be a trend indicator. While the trend sequence is maintained, for example rise, rise, fall, rise, rise, fall, the pattern of the indicator will continue to be repeated. When the pattern changes, as shown by the breaking of a trendline, then the trend has been broken, which usually implies a change in direction of the share price.

The overall impression of the RFI can be obtained from Figure 12.1. where the Allied Lyons share price and the indicator are shown. It can be seen that in general, major troughs and peaks in the share price are accompanied by troughs and peaks in the indicator. The scale of the chart is such that the detail of the RF indicator cannot be seen. In order to demonstrate the value of the indicator in signalling buying points, the portion of the chart around the trough at the end of 1988 is shown in larger scale in Figure 12.2. The detail in the RFI can now be seen clearly, and it consists of many more peaks and troughs than the share price itself. Because of this larger number of peaks and troughs, the simple approach to drawing a trendline, i.e. that two troughs or two peaks are sufficient to define it, would lead to a large number of trendlines and a correspondingly large number of false buying and selling signals. With the RF indicator, it is essential that a minimum of three peaks or three troughs must lie on the trendline

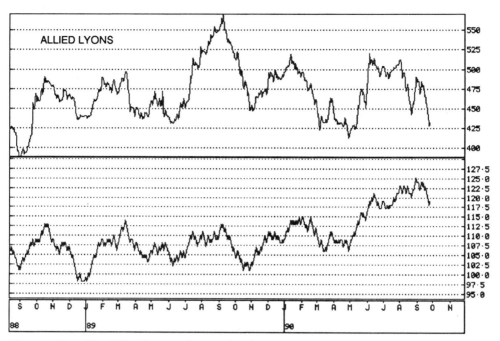

Figure 12.1. The Allied Lyons share price (upper panel) with the RFI (lower panel).

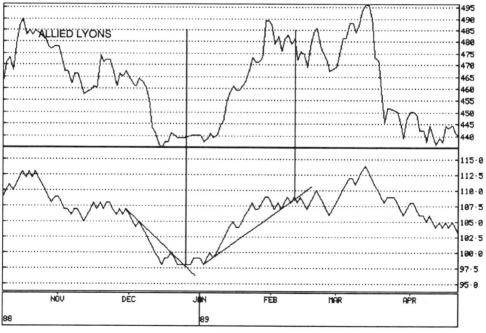

Figure 12.2. The buying and selling signals generated by the penetration of trend-lines by the RFI. The points at which the trends are broken are shown by the vertical lines.

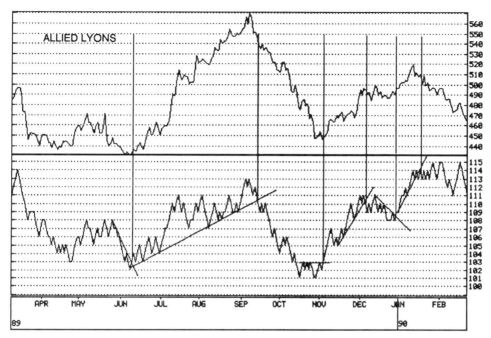

Figure 12.3. More buying and selling signals generated by the RFI(lower panel) of the Allied Lyons share price (upper panel).

before it becomes valid. This reduces the number of buying and selling signals enormously.

Using this approach to Figure 12.2, a downtrend line can be drawn in December 1988. This line is broken by the indicator on the 27th December 1988. The price at this point was 439p. Note how successful the indicator was in getting the investor into the share only marginally above the lowest price reached. Once the bottom had passed, it was possible to draw an uptrend line in January and February 1989. The RFI fell back down through this second trendline on the 10th February when the share price was 481p. This gave a gain of 9.6% before dealing costs for an investment lasting just under two months.

The most profitable move in the Allied Lyons share price over the last two years was the rise from early June 1989 which lasted until early September that year. This portion of the share price chart is shown in Figure 12.3. As shown, a trendline could be drawn from the end of May 1989, and the RFI broke through this on the 9th June, with the share price at 433p. Once again, the indicator was extremely successful in calling the turning point only a few days after the event while the price was still within a few percent of the low point. For the corresponding selling signal it can be seen that a lengthy trendline can be drawn with seven points lying on it. The selling signal came when the RFI turned down through this line on the 14th September 1989 when the price was 539p. This gave a profit excluding dealing costs of 24.5% in just three months!

The final useful rise in the Allied Lyons share price occurred from April/May 1990. This part of the share price chart is shown in Figure 12.4. As shown in the lower panel,

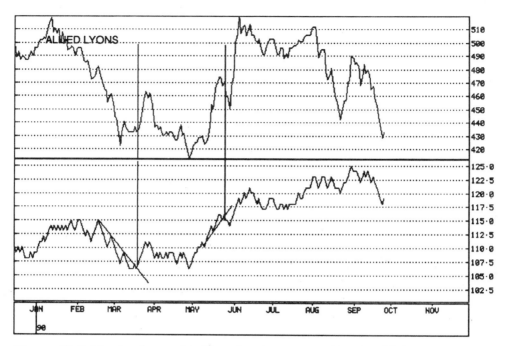

Figure 12.4. The buying and selling signals generated by the RFI(lower panel) of the Allied Lyons share price (upper panel) during 1990.

Table 12.1. The dates and prices for the buying and selling operations in Allied Lyons as signalled by the Rise- fall Index.

Date	Buy at	Date	Sell at	% Gain
27/12/88	439	10/02/88	481	9.6
09/06/89	433	14/09/89	539	24.5
03/11/89	417.5	07/12/89	491	17.6
29/12/89	496	18/01/90	500	0.8
20/03/90	435	25/05/90	459	3.2

a downtrend line can be drawn from the middle of February. The RFI rose through this trendline on the 20th March 1990 when the price was 435p. Although the price rose rapidly and then fell again, an uptrend line cannot be drawn at this point because there are not three troughs in a straight line. On the basis of the RFI therefore, the investor would have continued to hold the share through the dip in price in mid-April. From that point onwards an uptrend line in the RFI does develop. This line is broken by the RFI on the 25th May, when the price was 459p. Although this point still yielded a profit of

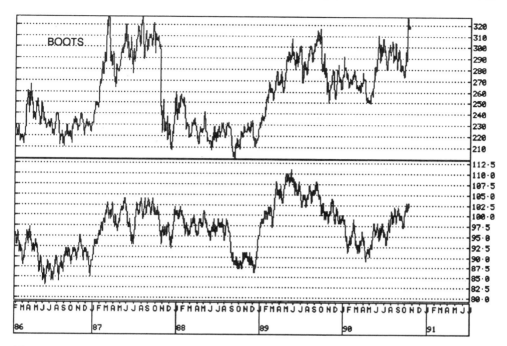

Figure 12.5. The Boots share price (upper panel) with the RFI (lower panel).

5.5% excluding dealing costs, this profit would be nearly all swallowed up by such costs. Thus the difficulty in this particular case is the premature selling signal which gets the investor out of the share about halfway up the rise. The buying and selling operations, with the gains from each transaction, are summarised in Table 12.1.

The case of Boots was discussed in the last Chapter as a useful test for indicators, since two profitable rises can be seen in the share price. One occurred from late 1986 and the other from the middle of 1988. The chart of the Boots price with the RSI is shown in Figure 12.5. This time there appears to be a very close correlation between the share price and the RSI.

Taking the rise which started in 1986, the expanded portion of the chart is shown in Figure 12.6. The successively lower series of peaks which form the downtrend line are seen quite clearly, there being four such peaks on the line. The RSI then rose through this line on the 13th June 1986 with the price at 228p. For investors who missed this first buying point, there was another chance only a few months later, since as can be seen another trendline could be drawn horizontally through the set of peaks which started in July 1986. The RSI rose through this second trendline on the 3rd September with the price at 223p. These buying signals bracket the short term double bottom formation which occurred in August. As can be seen by referring back to Figure 12.5, these buying signals were at levels which provided a good profit from the rise which took place during the rest of the year.

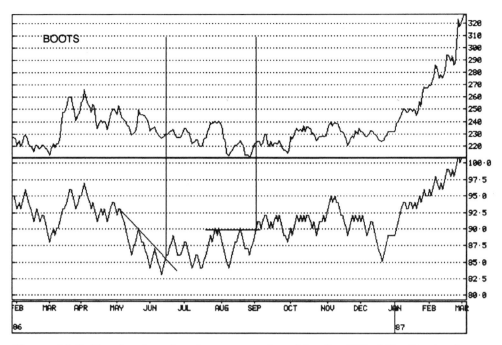

Figure 12.6. Two buying signals were produced by the RFI of the Boots share price during 1986.

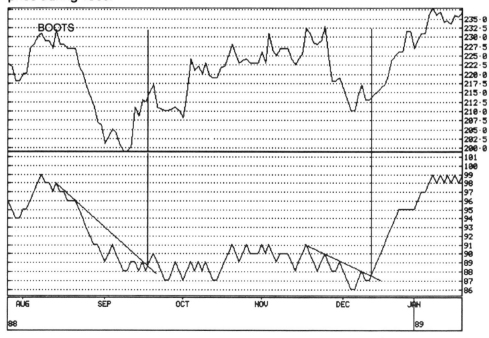

Figure 12.7. The buying signal produced by the RFI of the Boots share price during 1988.

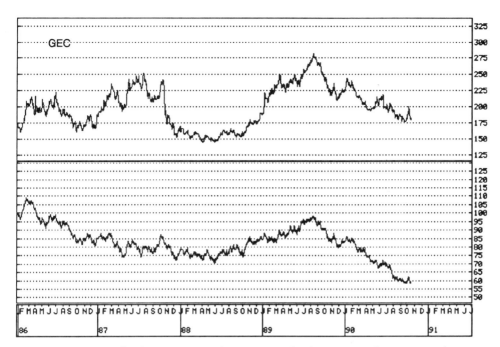

Figure 12.8. The GEC share price (upper panel) with the RFI (lower panel).

As far as the second rise in the Boots price is concerned, from Figure 12.5 it can be seen that the lowest share price was reached somewhere around the middle of 1988. The enlarged chart for the second half of 1988 is shown in Figure 12.7. Again, there are two buying opportunities, since a trendline can be drawn through the sharply falling RFI in August and again through the distinct peaks in late November 1988. In the first case the buying signal was given on the 20th September at 215p, while the second signal was given on the 13th December at 214p. Although the subsequent rise was not as large as that during the end of 1986, it still yielded a useful profit from either of these two buying signals.

GEC was shown to be a difficult case for developing a buying signal because of its rounded bottom formation. The chart plus the RFI is shown in Figure 12.8. At a glance, the RFI plot looks even worse than that of the share price, since it appears to be a rounded bottom formation which starts from the beginning of the plot. However, when enlarged to see the detail for most of 1988 as shown in Figure 12.9, the possibility of drawing trendlines then becomes more apparent. The first valid trendline which can be constructed is a horizontal one, starting in March 1988 and passing through five peaks. The RFI rose up through this trendline on the 20th April with the price standing at 151.5p. This is only a few percent above the low point on 15th April, and so once again the RFI method has been extremely successful in getting the investor in at a good price with a share which was rounding the bottom quite slowly.

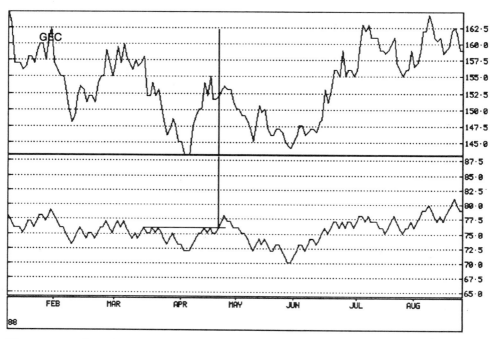

Figure 12.9. The GEC share price (upper panel) with the RFI (lower panel) during 1988. A buying signal is given by the RFI rising through the horizontal trendline.

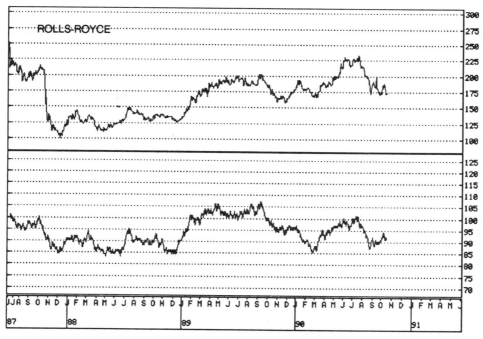

Figure 12.10. The Rolls-Royce share price (upper panel) with the RFI (lower panel).

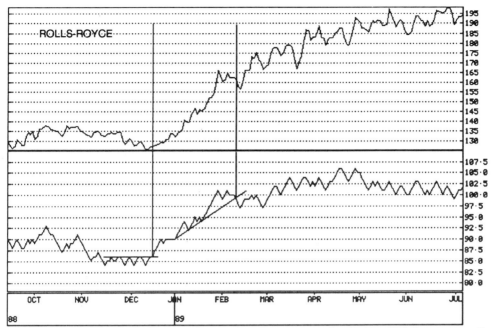

Figure 12.11. The Rolls-Royce share price (upper panel) with the RFI (lower panel) during 1988/89. A buying signal is given by the RFI rising through the horizontal trendline. A premature selling signal is given by the RFI penetrating the uptrend line.

In the case of Rolls-Royce, the need this time was for a selling signal because of the rounded top formation seen in Figure 12.10. The trough in the RFI in late 1988 suggested that there should have been a good buying signal at this point. The enlarged part of this chart in Figure 12.11 shows this to be the case. A good horizontal trendline can be drawn through the set of peaks which can be seen in the RFI in late November 1988. The RFI rises through this line on the 14th December 1988 with the price at 126.5p. During the rise in price that followed, it was possible to draw an uptrend line through the peaks occurring in January 1989, and the price rose through this line on the 9th February to generate a selling signal. This signal is quite obviously premature, since the at this point the rise is only halfway to the top. Thus the RFI method has not been particularly successful in this difficult case.

Although as we have shown, there are occasions where the RFI method generates late selling signals, it is much more useful as a generator of buying signals, and the examples given in this Chapter should serve to illustrate the power of this indicator.

CHAPTER 13

CHANNEL ANALYSIS

The envelope method was first described by J.M. Hurst in the United States in 1970 and has since been developed here in the UK into the technique now known as Channel Analysis (CA). The name is derived from the fact that share prices can be shown to remain within channels of constant depth, and a fairly simple analysis of the share price data will provide all of the information necessary to draw these channels.

The CA technique is an extremely powerful method for determining the most probable course of the share price over the near future, taking into account the degree of randomness inherent in share price movement. It will alert the investor to the probability that a trend in the share price will change direction within this future time window, so that the investor is well placed to take advantage of the change once it has been confirmed.

Note the above emphasis on confirmation that a change in direction has occurred. CA is a probability based method that takes into account the cyclical predictable components and the unpredictable random components of share prices. CA therefore signals that it is highly probable that a trend will change direction at a certain point in the near future, but there is still a finite possibility that the direction will change sooner or later than this. The Gulf crisis is a prime example of an unforeseen random event with a particularly depressing effect on world stock markets. Waiting for confirmation of a predicted change will prevent the investor from jumping in too soon and be carried along in the wrong direction by an adverse trend that seems never-ending.

The use of terms such as 'probability based','predictable cyclical components' and the like may give the impression that a degree in mathematics or statistics is necessary before an investor can begin to understand or take advantage of Channel Analysis. Nothing could be further from the truth, since excellent results can be obtained with nothing more than a chart of a share price and a pencil. In other words, channel analysis is an ideal techniques for those investors who are inclined towards charting methods in general.

Fundamental Principles of Channel Analysis

The guiding principles of the CA technique can be encapsulated in a number of observations:

- Share price movement contains both random and cyclical components.
- A channel of constant depth can be drawn so that the share price will penetrate the channel boundaries on only a few occasions. The depth

should be the minimum possible commensurate with the restriction on boundary penetration.

- The channel can be projected a limited distance into the future. Future price movement will obey the same rules as past movement, i.e. the vast majority of the movement will be contained within the channel.

- When the share price approaches the upper or lower boundary of the channel, there is a high probability that it will reverse direction.

- The shape of the channel is due to cycles, i.e. trends, in the share price of periodicity greater than the periodicity of the channel.

- The price movement within the channel is due to random movement and the effect of cycles, i.e. trends, of periodicity equal to or less than that of the channel itself.

- Further channels can be constructed outside of existing channels. The rule then is that the outer channel should be constructed with the minimum depth possible subject to the restriction that the inner channel should not penetrate the outer channel, but should touch it on just a few occasions.

- The advantage of using several channels nested within each other is that they can be drawn so as to represent short-term, medium-term and long-term trends. The investor will then be able to estimate for how long a particular trend will persist before it is forced to change direction by a more dominant longer term trend.

With a computer system these channels will be drawn automatically such as to obey the rules for penetration by prices and other channels, and the Figures in this chapter are produced in this way.. For the pencil and paper investor, it will be found that only a small amount of practice is necessary in order that channels can be drawn by eye with a high degree of accuracy.

A useful starting point for a discussion of the power of channel analysis is the Allied Lyons share price. By using the rules listed above, two channels have been drawn on the chart of the share price since 1984, as shown in Figure 13.1. The inner channel was drawn first of all so as to reflect the many rises and falls which occurred over the period of the chart. The outer channel was then drawn so as to accommodate the large rise and fall in 1987 and the peak in the middle of 1989. It can be seen that the outer channel has to be made to turn downwards since the peak in 1989, otherwise the lower boundary would violate the troughs at the beginning of 1990. Such concerns are vital if correct channels are to be drawn.

A much better appreciation of the way the price oscillates inside the inner channel and the way in which the inner channel oscillates within the outer channel can be obtained from the enlarged part of the chart shown in Figure 13.2. Now it is clear that the crash of 1987 was just a modest correction of the Allied Lyons share price which just took the price a small distance across the inner channel boundaries.

The usefulness of channel analysis in generating a buying signal in 1988 can be seen by the expanded portion of the chart as it would have been drawn in late August 1988

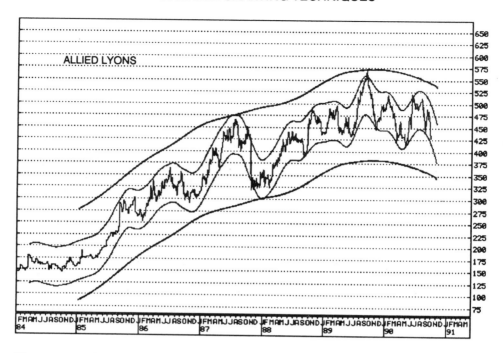

Figure 13.1. Inner and outer channels drawn around the Allied Lyons share price.

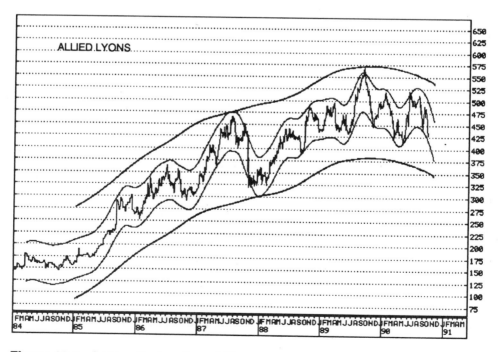

Figure 13.2. A magnified portion of Figure 13.1.

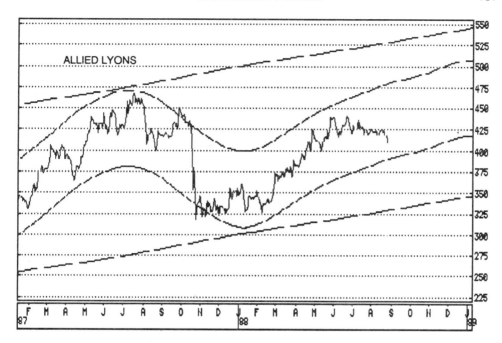

Figure 13.3. Approaching a buying point for Allied Lyons in August 1988.

(Figure 13.3). The most reasonable projection of the upper boundary of the inner channel is that which just brushes the series of peaks in May and June. Since the channel depth must be kept constant, the lower boundary is now also defined. We can see that in Figure 13.3 the price is falling towards the lower boundary of the inner channel. Channel analysis now leads us to expect a bounce back of the share price from this lower boundary, and judged by the position of the share price this bounce back is very imminent. We are therefore expecting a reversal of the price fall soon, and this will be a signal to buy. Channel analysis does much more than simply generate buying and selling signals. It also gives us a very good indication of the extent of the future price rise or price fall. In Figure 13.3. we can see the upper boundary of the outer channel, which has been transferred from the small scale chart. We expect the inner boundary to bounce back from this, and at the present rate of climb of the inner channel this should happen by the end of 1988. Since the level of the upper boundary of the outer channel at that time will be in the range 480p to 500p, this gives us an expectation of about 100p for the price rise following the bounce back which is imminent.

As shown in Figure 13.4, the price formed two small troughs at the level of the predicted lower boundary of the inner channel. The first trough was at a price of 390p on the 1st September 1988, and as soon as the price rose from this level the share could be bought with reasonable confidence. A good buying point would have been on the 5th September at 394p.

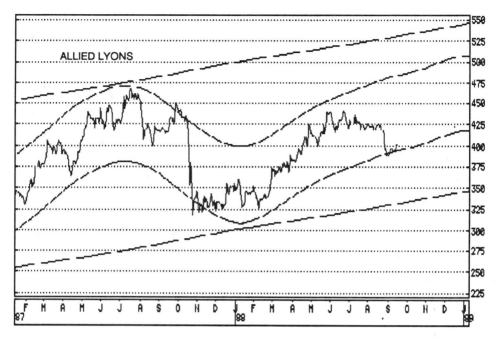

Figure 13.4. The buying point is now signalled by a rise from the position of the lower boundary.

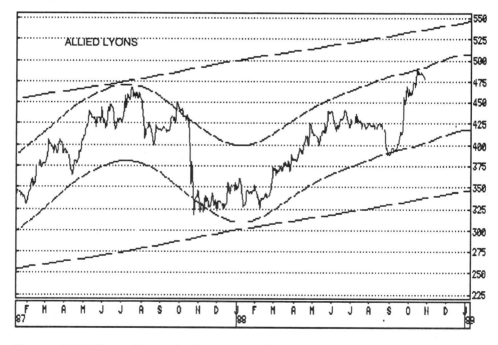

Figure 13.5. The selling point is now signalled by a fall from the position of the upper boundary.

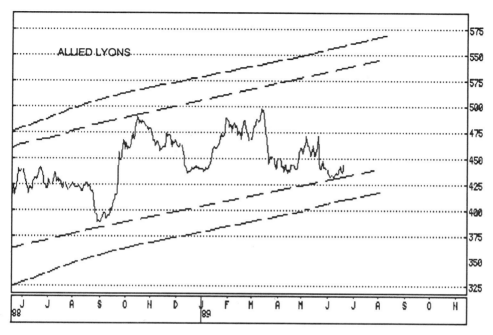

Figure 13.6 . The buying point in mid-1989 is signalled by a rise from the position of the lower boundary.

The corresponding selling point is determined by a similar approach, and while the price is rising, an ultimate target of 480 to 500p is already predicted as discussed above. The price reached 490p on the 17th October 1988 and then fell back as shown in Figure 13.5. At this point therefore it was time to sell the share, at a price of 485p for a gain in just two months of 23%.

The largest rise in the Allied Lyons share price occurred in mid-1989. The position in June 1989 is shown in Figure 13.6. The inner channel had reached the projected lower boundary of the outer channel, and therefore the expectation was for a rebound of the inner channel, which of course means a rebound of the share price. The share price reached a trough on the 8th June 1989 at 431p and then bounced up. The most conservative approach is to wait for the next trough to see if this is at a higher level than the previous one. If so, then the lower boundary must have begun to move up. The rise in price from the low point on the 13th June 1989 defined this low point of 434p on the 14th June as being the required second trough, and so the share could then be bought at a price of 439p.

The price then rose quite sharply towards the projected upper boundary of the outer channel, and by the 17th July 1989 when the price fell back slightly from that of the previous day, any reasonable investor would have considered that it was time to sell. The price obtained would have been 507p, for a gain of 15.4%. Although the price then recovered and rose even further, this has to be considered to be an overshoot of the

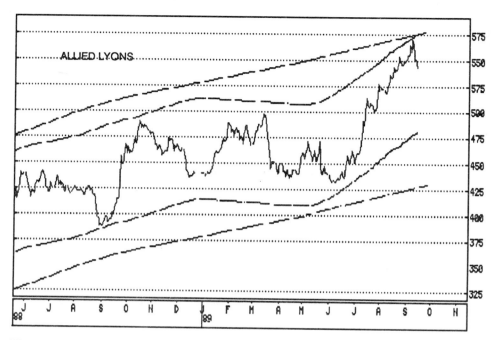

Figure 13.7 . The selling point in 1989 is signalled by a fall from the projected position of the upper boundary of the outer channel.

projected channel as shown in Figure 13.7, and channel analysis would not have kept the investor in until this point.

Finally in the Allied Lyons case, it was shown earlier that moving averages would have generated a buying and selling signal for the rise that occurred in the second quarter of 1990. Figure 13.8 shows the position of channels at the beginning of April 1990. The price was rapidly falling towards the conjunction of the projected lower boundaries of the inner and outer channels, and therefore a bounce back was highly likely. The lowest point was reached on the 27th April 1990 and the price then rose before falling again. The rise on the 10th May defined the price of 423p on the previous day as being the second trough. Since this trough was at a higher level than the trough on the 27th April this is therefore a strong indication that the lower boundary of the inner channel has turned up. The share could have been bought at this point for 424p.

The rise in price from this point was so rapid that the projected upper boundary of the inner channel was reached in less than two months. As before , the investor would wait for a fall back from the position of the upper boundary, hoping of course that this was not one of those occasions where the fall back is too rapid to get in near the top price. This was not the case here, and the investor would have been able to get out on the 6th June 1990 at a price of around 507p.

Although channel analysis is an extremely powerful technique, it is unable, as is any other technique, to deal with the random, totally unexpected price movement. As was

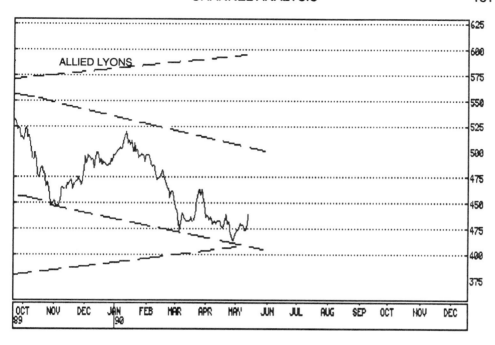

Figure 13.8 . The buying point point in 1990 is signalled by a rise from the projected position of the lower boundary of the inner channel.

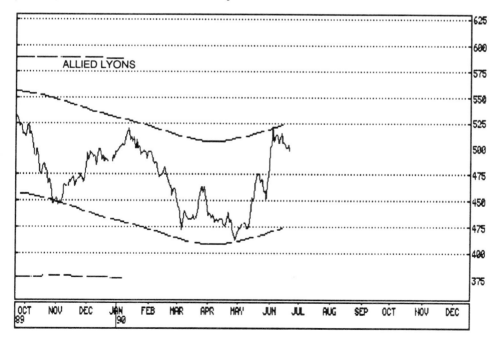

Figure 13.9 . The selling point in 1990 is signalled by a fall from the projected position of the upper boundary of the inner channel.

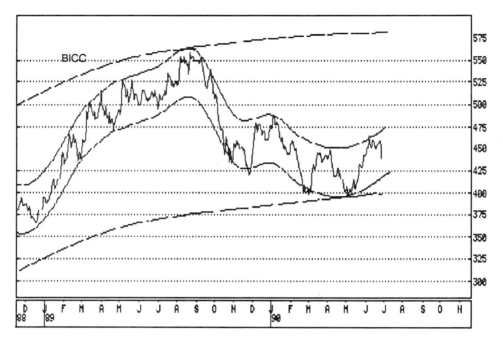

Figure 13.10 . The buying point point for BICC in 1990 is signalled by a rise from the projected position of the lower boundary of the inner channel.

discussed at the beginning of this book, and will be mentioned again in the conclusion, the only way to protect against adverse movements of this nature is by means of a stop loss. As a good example of the unexpected, the case of BICC is shown in the following few charts.

The fall back from the peak in the price reached in mid-1989 appeared to be slowing down by early 1990. As can be seen from Figure 13.10, the inner channel had passed through a series of cyclical movements, the lowest one of which appeared to be that formed in April/May 1990. The price rose from this level for several weeks before falling back again. However, the peak formed by this latest rise was higher than the peak in the previous cycle in March. This of necessity forced the upper boundary of the outer channel to turn up, with its low point therefore coinciding with the low point of the inner channel during April/May.

From this analysis, as the price fell back during June, it was expected that it would soon reach the now rising outer boundary and bounce back up. This point would be expected to be any time between late June and mid-August. In the event, the price reached the projected level of the outer channel lower boundary at 423p on the 29th June 1990, bounced back slightly, fell back to the boundary again on the 10th of July and then rose again the next day, 11th July. At this point it seemed that all signals were at go for a rise in price, and investors would have been buying at this point as shown in Figure 13.11.

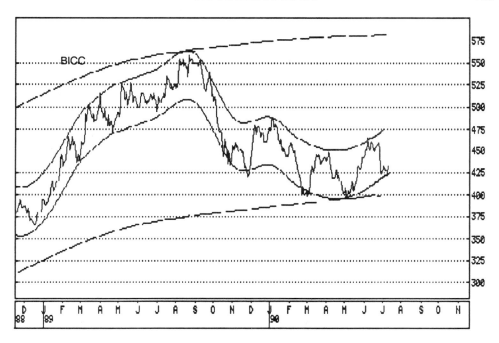

Figure 13.11. The BICC share price bounced up from the lower boundary of the inner channel on the 11th July 1990, signalling a buying point.

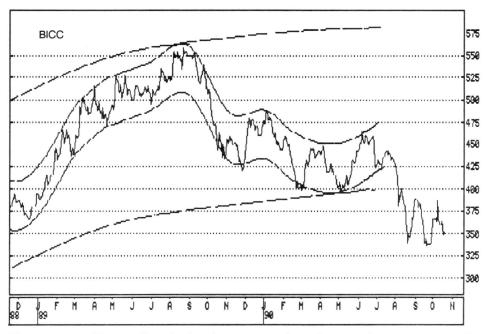

Figure 13.12. The predicted price rise was caught up by a random movement taking the BICC share price well below the projected channel.

For the next few days the price rose and then began to fall again. The investor would not be unduly worried at this point, because the price would be expected to bounce up again once the now rising lower boundary of the inner channel was reached. This did seem to be the case in mid-July, since the price rose from the level of the boundary. However, this turned out to be a false dawn, since the price fell once again in a sustained move that was also caught up in the Gulf crisis. The price fell down to 380p before a modest recovery which rapidly petered out.

Adverse and totally unpredictable movements such as these, soon after a buying operation has been carried out, can easily be protected against by a stop loss which is geared to the channel analysis technique. This is easily done by keeping a level a few percent below the predicted lower boundary of the inner channel. Then, as was the case above with BICC, as soon as the price falls down through the projected channel and reaches the rising stop loss level, the share should be sold. Such an approach will limit the damage caused to just a few percent, and this will easily be recovered by the subsequent profitable investments.

CHAPTER 14

CONCLUSION

The following rules were first put forward in the book 'Channel Analysis', and have been modified slightly because of the differing subject matter of this book.

The main way in which investors lose money is to fail to admit that they have made a mistake, and thereby fail to cut short a losing position early on before substantial losses have accumulated. If investors can overcome this psychological problem, they shift the balance of probabilities even more in their favour, because they will allow their profits to run while minimising their losses. Failure to maintain discipline at all times will totally negate the powerful techniques which have been presented in this book. Some guideline rules which should help the investor to maintain this discipline are presented in the following pages.

CAPITAL MUST BE PRESERVED AT ALL COSTS

This is the first and overriding rule of stock market investment, and the remaining rules and comments are designed so that this first rule can be followed consistently. The natural consequence of this rule is that when a position has been taken in a share, the investor must get out as soon as it is obvious that the share price is misbehaving. There will always be another opportunity for making profit. The prevention of loss is as important as the achievement of profit. Remember there is no such thing as a paper loss. All losses are real.

NEVER ACT SOLELY ON ADVICE

Besides the internal pressure to stray from this disciplined path caused by investor psychology, the external pressures from the investment industry are immense. The investor is constantly bombarded with advice from stockbrokers, junk mail and the media. Some of the most successful investors read nothing but the share prices page in their newspaper and do not even glance at the rest of the business section. I would not go quite as far as this, since a feel for the general investment climate which can be gained from these pages can be extremely valuable. By all means listen to advice from whatever source, but never, never act on it without analysing the data by the methods discussed in this book and then act only if the analysis is favourable.

NEVER PUT MORE THAN ONE EIGHTH OF YOUR CAPITAL IN ONE SHARE

However positively the investor feels about the potential for a particular share, this positive feeling must be tempered by knowledge of the existence of random movement.

Because of this, the investor should not, and must not, have 100% confidence in any one given situation. The temptation to go for broke and put everything into one magic share is always at the back of the investor's mind, and that is where it should stay. Never, never commit more than one eighth of the investment capital to one share. This will keep the risk as low as possible while maintaining the potential for profit. From time to time there will be occasions when it is not possible to find eight shares in which to invest. In such cases put the money into short-term interest bearing accounts where it can be got at instantly when the need arises.

DO NOT ANTICIPATE SHARE PRICE TURNING POINTS

We should never make an investment until after the change in direction of the trend has been confirmed, and we should never disinvest until the change in direction has been confirmed. The profit available in upward trends which we buy into shortly after the start of these new trends is such that we do not need to worry about squeezing an extra one or two percentage points out by trying to anticipate them.

PROTECT PROFITS BY STOP-LOSSES

Just as it is not necessary to try to squeeze extra gain out of a trend by jumping the gun, so it is not necessary to try to squeeze extra gain by continuing to run after the finishing tape has been passed. In the majority of cases, the termination of an upward trend results in a sudden sharp reversal of price over the course of one or two days. The risk increases dramatically as the inner channel increases in upward slope. Although we have shown by channel analysis that we can determine the selling point closely in time, it is essential that we protect ourselves against the conjunction of an adverse random movement and a change in direction of short term cycles. This can only be done by using one of the various stop-loss methods discussed in Chapter 1. It is better to sell prematurely than to lose profit by staying invested too long in a share which is reaching its peak price.

PROTECT AGAINST LOSSES BY STOP-LOSSES

This would appear to mean the same as the previous heading, but here we mean the stop-loss to apply not to the profitable position above, but to the case where an incorrect buying decision has been made and the share starts to fall in price instead of rising. In this case the position never was in profit. Even so, the rule about protection of capital is paramount. The temptation is to think that we were slightly premature in recognising the start of the upward trend, and that in a few more days or weeks the expected trend will materialise. This attitude is a major cause of stock market losses, and must never be adopted. Never forget that if we can reduce our losses to say four or five percent, including dealing costs, when we make a bad decision, then this is only four or five percent of one eighth of our total capital. We can afford to experience theoretically twenty or twenty-five such losses before one eighth of our capital is wiped out, and one hundred and sixty to two hundred such losses before we are totally wiped out. The chances of such this happening are at vanishing point for the conservative investment philosophy policy we are advocating in this book.

STAY WITH ALPHA SHARES

The influence of dealing costs on profit is quite large when compounded over a number of transactions. The spread of prices, i.e. the difference between buying and selling prices for a share are part of this equation. The spread is at a minimum for the alpha shares, and there is usually plenty of opportunity for finding a share amongst these 120-130 shares which is approaching an upward trend. If not, then of course move down a level to the beta shares, of which there are many more, but where the spread will be greater. It should not be necessary to move to gamma shares other than in exceptional circumstances.

IGNORE DIVIDENDS

Dividends are nice to receive, and if the investor is fully invested in eight different shares for most of the year, he can expect to receive many dividends which will add to his profit. That is all that can be said about them, for the investor should never let an impending dividend affect his buying or selling operation. In other words, if the signal comes to sell, do not think of hanging on for a little longer because the dividend will be announced the following week. If a buying point is approaching, do not buy in before the change in direction is confirmed simply because a dividend will be captured.

KEEP TRACK OF THE MARKET

It is always essential that the general investment climate is tracked by means of a market indicator such as the FT30 Index, the FT All Share Index or the FTSE100 Index. Weekly values are sufficient to do this. In view of the increasing tendency of London to follow slavishly the gyrations of Wall Street, it is also a good idea to keep track of the Dow Jones Index on a weekly basis. Short term dramatic movements in the US market almost always cause an effect in the London market. If the market is falling, adopt a more cautious stance towards your existing holdings and new purchases, and watch your stop losses very carefully. The investor may well find that in the initial stages it is very difficult to stick to this investment philosophy. He may find that straying off this narrow path brings him an instant reward that he would otherwise have missed. This is just the quixotic nature of the world of probability. Over a number of years the investor following these guidelines will see his capital gaining steadily in value, while the investor who allows himself to be diverted from time to time will be subjecting himself to increasing risk that will inevitably take its toll. Finally, the investor who has successfully followed these techniques for perhaps a year or so will begin to look for greater gains than those which can be made out of investment in shares. Then, and not before, is the time to turn to the magnifying effect of dealing in traded options. In inexperienced hands traded options can be unacceptably risky, but can be extremely rewarding when they are thoroughly understood and when the investor is correct about the movement of the underlying security. Traded Options Simplified (see Appendix) will take the beginner from the basics through to simple strategies and then on to advanced strategies, as well as discussing some powerful new techniques for investors familiar with the field.

Appendix

Addresses

For lists of brokers: The Secretary, The Stock Exchange, London EC2.

Other Books by the Author

Stocks and Shares Simplified, ISBN 0-471-92131-0 Published by John Wiley & Sons Ltd., Chichester.

Traded Options Simplified, ISBN 1-871857-00-7 Published by Qudos Publications, distributed by John Wiley & Sons Ltd.

Channel Analysis, ISBN 1-871857-02-3 Published by Qudos Publications, distributed by John Wiley & Sons Ltd.

Chart Books

Chart books of the alpha shares and others are obtainable from Qudos Publications, 16 Queensgate, Bramhall, Cheshire, SK7 1JT. Tel: 061-439-3926.

Historical Data

Closing prices of all alpha shares since 1983 are obtainable in printed form (ISBN 1-871857-01-5) or on floppy disk in a variety of formats from Qudos Publications at the above address.

Microcomputer Software

The charts in this book were produced by the Synergy Software Technical Analyst and Channel Analysis packages. For further information contact: Synergy Software, Britannic House, 20 Dunstable Road, Luton, LU1 1ED. Tel: 0582-424282